The Eurasian Connection

**DIRECTIONS IN DEVELOPMENT**
Trade

# The Eurasian Connection

*Supply-Chain Efficiency along the Modern Silk Route through Central Asia*

Cordula Rastogi and Jean-François Arvis

**THE WORLD BANK**
Washington, D.C.

ISBN (paper): 978-0-8213-9912-5
ISBN (electronic): 978-0-8213-9913-2
DOI: 10.1596/978-0-8213-9912-5

*Cover photo:* © Debra H. Malovany. Used with permission. Further permission required for reuse.
*Cover design:* Debra Naylor, Naylor Design, Inc.

**Library of Congress Cataloging-in-Publication data has been requested.**

# Contents

## Boxes

## Figures

# Foreword

One of the defining features of the twenty-first century could be the economic integration of the Eurasian supercontinent from the Pacific to the Atlantic, and from the Arctic Sea to the Indian Ocean. Distances are huge, mountains and deserts constitute formidable barriers, and population densities are low in large parts of Eurasia. But the forces of global integration, the improvements in communication and reductions in transport costs, and the growth and prosperity of the regional economies of Asia and Europe constitute drivers that will push continental economic integration forward in Eurasia. If history is a guide, the greatest risk to this integration process stems from geopolitical, regional, and subregional political rivalries.

Central Asia lies at the heart of the Eurasian land mass. Many of the communications routes that will connect Asia and Europe run through Central Asia. Long seen as hampered by their "land-locked" status, Central Asian countries can benefit in the future from becoming "land-linked" by connecting with the large economies of their rapidly growing or already prosperous neighbors, especially China, India, the Gulf countries, Russia, and Europe. And Central Asia can benefit from the Eurasian transit traffic and trade that should develop in the coming decades.

As this volume demonstrates, the Eurasian economic integration process has been under way since the fall of the Iron and Bamboo Curtains and has already affected the countries of Central Asia. But the study also makes abundantly clear that much remains to be done if this integration process is to unfold fully and bring the benefits of connectivity that have so strongly supported the rapid growth of the global economy, and especially of East Asia in recent decades.

This study explains how supply chain fragmentation remains a serious obstacle to economic development of Central Asia and to Eurasian integration more generally. It provides a comprehensive assessment of the various factors that yet impede supply-chain integration, including weak transport and communications infrastructure, but as important, and perhaps more so, critical weaknesses in policy, institutions, and governance. Based on this assessment this report provides an insightful set of recommendations that, if taken up by the governments of Central Asia and by their key neighbors, would go a long way in promoting the effective integration of Central Asia into an increasingly connected Eurasian continental economy and with that into the global economy.

Johannes F. Linn                        Hans Timmer
*Brookings Institution and*              *Chief Economist*
*Emerging Markets Forum*                 *Europe and Central Asia Region*
                                         *World Bank*

# Preface

This book is not the first attempt to review the challenge of reconstructing supply chains in Central Asia after the collapse of the Soviet Union. However, the perspective differs from the prevalent vision based on development of transport corridors. Many initiatives supported by different institutions such as the Central Asia Regional Economic Cooperation (CAREC) Program[1] or the Transport Corridor Europe-Caucasus-Asia (TRACECA) Program[2] have focused on improvements of specific and eventually competing routes. Here, the focus is on supply-chain performance, global or regional connectivity, and a full set of enabling measures to foster these outcomes.

This perspective also includes a wide range of issues at the national or regional level—regulations, delivery of private services, institutions, and organizations or partnerships, most of which are not corridor-specific. More importantly, the book aims to provide a new understanding of challenges to connectivity in Central Asia, given the new dynamics in the region. Because Kazakhstan in many respects is considered to be the pivot of Central Asia, recent issues include the implications of the Eurasian Customs Union for trade and transport facilitation. The fast growth of trade in western China, foremost in Xinjiang Province, with goods mostly transported through Kazakhstan, is also a historic development. The supply-chain connectivity paradigm and the inclusion of the new environment imply a revision of the classical set of policy recommendations. Rather than bringing entirely new ideas, the ambition here is to provide a new prioritization of recommendations and revisit the solutions for implementation.

The document is organized as follows: Chapter 1 introduces the reader to the old and modern Silk Route, and chapter 2 reviews Central Asia's trade potential. Chapters 3 and 4 look, respectively, at Euro-Asian transit and regional connections by road and rail. Chapter 5 revisits the evidence of supply-chain inefficiencies. Chapter 6 tracks the causes of national and cross-border policy constraints, operational constraints, or markets. The final chapter outlines the opportunities and enabling measures to establish reliable connections.

## Notes

1. The CAREC Program, led by the Asian Development Bank (ADB), is a partnership of 10 countries (Afghanistan, Azerbaijan, China, Kazakhstan, the Kyrgyz Republic, Mongolia, Pakistan, Tajikistan, Turkmenistan, and Uzbekistan) supported by six

multilateral institutions, working together to promote cooperative development leading to accelerated growth and poverty reduction.

2. The TRACECA Program was initiated in May 1993, involving ministries of trade and transport from eight countries: Armenia, Azerbaijan, Georgia, Kazakhstan, Kyrgyzstan (now the Kyrgyz Republic), Tajikistan, Turkmenistan, and Uzbekistan.

# Acknowledgments

The preparation of this report was led by Cordula Rastogi (senior transport economist, PRMTR), under the guidance of Philippe Le Houerou (VP ECA), Indermit Gill (director DCDP, former chief economist, ECA), Hans Timmer (chief economist, ECA), Willem van Eeghen (lead economist, ECA), Henry Kerali (country director, ECCU3, former sector manager, ECSTR), Saroj Kumar Jha (country director, ECCU9), Mona Haddad (sector manager, PRMTR), and Juan Gaviria (sector manager, ECSTR).

The main authors of the report are Cordula Rastogi (senior transport economist, PRMTR, formerly ECSTR) and Jean-François Arvis (senior transport economist, PRMTR).

Many colleagues at the World Bank provided major inputs and reviewed the results or provided materials, including Rodrigo Archondo-Callao (senior highway engineer, ECSTR), Karlygash Dairabayeva (consultant, PRMTR), and Daniel Saslavsky (trade specialist, PRMTR). Several trade facilitation and transport experts contributed major insights or findings, including John Arnold, Dick Bullock, Vasile Olievschki, Tapio Naula, Oleg Samukhin, and John Winner. The authors also thank the peer reviewers: Marc Juhel, Johannes Linn, and Ekaterine T. Vashakmadze.

# Abbreviations

| | |
|---|---|
| ADB | Asian Development Bank |
| ADR | Agreement Concerning the International Carriage of Dangerous Goods by Road |
| ATP | Agreement on the International Carriage of Perishable Foodstuffs and on the Special Equipment to Be Used for Such Carriage |
| CAREC | Central Asia Regional Economic Cooperation |
| CC | Customs Code |
| CCC | Customs Control Committee (Kazakhstan) |
| CCTT | Coordinating Council on Transsiberian Transportation |
| CIS | Commonwealth of Independent States |
| CMR | Convention on the Contract for the International Carriage of Goods by Road |
| CPMM | CAREC Corridor Performance Measurement and Monitoring |
| CU | Customs Union |
| CUC | Customs Union Commission |
| DB | Deutsche Bahn |
| EEC | Eurasian Economic Commission |
| EU | European Union |
| EurAsEC | Eurasian Economic Community |
| FEU | forty-foot equivalent unit |
| FSU | former Soviet Union |
| GDP | gross domestic product |
| GM | General Motors |
| GNI | gross national income |
| ICBC | International Centre of Boundary Cooperation, Khorgos |
| IRU | International Road Transport Union |
| KR | Kyrgyz Republic |
| KTZ | Kazakhstan Temir Jolu (Kazakhstan Railways) |
| LPI | Logistics Performance Index |
| NATO | North Atlantic Treaty Organization |

| | |
|---|---|
| NELTI | New Eurasian Land Transport Initiative |
| OSJD | Organization for Cooperation of Railways |
| RK | Republic of Kazakhstan |
| RZD | Russian Railways |
| SCO | Shanghai Cooperation Organization |
| SMGS | Agreement on International Goods Traffic by Rail |
| TEU | twenty-foot equivalent unit |
| TIR | Transports Internationaux Routiers (International Road Transport) |
| TKR | Trans-Kazakhstan Railways |
| TRACECA | Transport Corridor Europe-Caucasus-Asia |
| TSR | Trans-Siberian Railways |
| UNECE | United Nations Economic Commission for Europe |
| UNESCAP | UN Economic and Social Commission for Asia and the Pacific |
| XUAR | Xingjian-Uighur Autonomous Region |

# Overview

Central Asia is often associated with the Silk Route or Road, the longest overland trade route connecting China to Europe and one of the oldest in history. Modern Central Asia comprises five independent republics: Kazakhstan, the Kyrgyz Republic, Tajikistan, Turkmenistan, and Uzbekistan.[1] These land transport routes, often referred to as the Eurasian land bridge, help this deeply landlocked region connect over long distances to its trading partners. Growth opportunities and the future prosperity of the region are highly dependent upon the efficiency of its internal and external supply-chain connections, which is the focus of this report. What matters for supply chains that connect importers and exporters is more than just a physical link or path on a map.

Most Eurasian trade goes by ship through the Suez Canal, with a throughput of 40 million twenty-foot equivalent units (TEUs) for containers and 500 million tons of bulk merchandise in 2012. The rail link between China and Europe is currently enjoying renewed interest because it may offer competitive trade-offs between costs and time over the maritime route. Several multinational companies have started to operate regular container "block" trains on this route through the Russian Federation and Kazakhstan, or through a competing northern route through Siberia and Manchuria. However, the land bridge cannot—and likely will never—compete in volume because its potential throughput is only 1–2 percent of what is now carried by sea. It may well establish itself not as a substitute but as a complement to shipping to increase the reliability of time-sensitive supply chains involving manufacturing production sharing, such as high-value components in the automotive or computer industries.

Even more than the production-sharing business opportunities in the globalized world, trade and transport links are essential to sustain regional economies in the Central Asian republics. This is because of not only their dependence on Europe and China for trade in Asian imports and exports, but also to promote local added-value and trade opportunities between themselves, as was the case in ancient times. The five Central Asian countries host a combined population of about 40 million. Russian Siberia and the province of Xinjiang in western China, also part of the modern Silk Route, have about 20 million each.

Supply-chain connectivity depends on the quality of the infrastructure on specific routes. However, even more important are countrywide factors such as quality and sophistication of services, customs and border control, and related trade or transportation policies that affect logistics performance. Beyond national policies cross-border cooperation is also essential to harmonize the logistics regulations and facilitate international supply chains, especially for landlocked countries such as in Central Asia, which depend on each other to trade globally. Ultimately, supply chains are only as strong as their weakest link, so progress made in infrastructure may not compensate for a lack of progress or slower progress in other areas such as the quality of logistics services and trade facilitation.

The paradox of the modern Silk Route is that despite changes in transport technology its governance and organization are reminiscent of the old Silk Road. The latter depended on fragmented caravan trade. No direct business connection was in place between buyers and sellers, and trade happened through a long and costly series of sales in the famous trading cities along the route. Today, supply-chain fragmentation still weakens links and reduces the efficiency of supply chains. Intrusive border controls, local intermediaries, unreliable transport services by rail or road, and inadequate infrastructure keep supply chains fragmented in that the principal (shipper or global logistics company) does not have a full control of what happens in transit: shipments can be delayed by weeks, and security concerns are sometimes alarming.

The reliance on long transit routes for all types of trade is one source of complexity and fragmentation: In the case of Uzbekistan, for example, goods have to flow in transit through Russia, China, and Kazakhstan to reach Uzbekistan. Another source of complexity and fragmentation is a result of past history and comes from the organization of trade set in place after the collapse of the Soviet Union. Until very recently, the design of supply chains has been developed country-by-country, with, on the one hand, a strong focus on control rather than trade facilitation, and, on the other hand, the protection of local services (brokers and truckers). Regional trade and transit flows are also hampered by regional political considerations, which may create even more obstacles at borders.

## Moving on a Connectivity Agenda

Improving connectivity (box O.1) and reducing the fragmentation of supply chains implies a renewed push for national improvements and cross-border integration in such areas as infrastructure standards, trade facilitation, and service regulation. This complex set of tasks outlined in the next section requires decisive collective action.

Governments in Central Asia are aware of the importance of the agenda, but so far few consistent actions have been taken, both within countries as well as between countries. Silos of administrative responsibilities in transition economies do not help tackle cross-cutting topics such as the underlying logistics chains to support importers and exporters. It means that incentives of independent agencies are not aligned with the collective action of improving

---

**Box O.1 What Is Supply-Chain Connectivity?**

The reference to connectivity in the context of logistics has been popularized by the World Bank report on logistics performance *Connecting to Compete: Trade Logistics in the Global Economy* (World Bank 2007). In this context supply-chain connectivity is the ability of the traders in one country to effectively establish reliable supply chains with their customers or suppliers. These supply chains are not taking one specific route or mode of transportation, but rather have several options. Their performance is dependent not only on the transport route but also on the logistics business environment, which depends on national or regional patterns (customs is a nationwide agency). The criterion may depend on the product.

For instance, exporters of dried fruits from the Isfara region in northern Tajikistan are dependent on partnerships with long-distance road services with Russia and Europe to serve their customers and face potential issues in transit. They are also dependent on the local cross-border road network within the Kyrgyz Republic to expand and diversify their collection area. In the case of the General Motors factory in Uzbekistan, or a large wholesaler operating from Almaty, the concern will be the predictability of the rail transit to Almaty and beyond from distant sources in East Asia, Russia, or the European Union, so as to avoid potential stock-outs.

---

supply chains: for instance, ministries of transportation are incentivized to build infrastructure rather than to improve the quality of services or to open national markets to foreign providers.

To address some of these coordination issues, for example, the government of Kazakhstan has set up an interagency committee on logistics in 2012. Kazakhstan, given its size and geographical position, has to play a leading role in the implementation of such policies.

The private sector has a key role in helping move the connectivity agenda. Unfortunately, the region lacks a strong, organized base of export-oriented manufacturers, due to the commodity-oriented structure of production. The demand for reform and pressure on governments has therefore not been fueled by a public-private debate on national logistics efficiency as in Asian countries. Probably a remnant of the Soviet era, logistics is associated with suppliers of logistics. The voice of the private sector is carried by typically quasi-administrative business association representatives of local truckers, forwarders, and customs brokers/representatives. Unlike in Europe or Asia, very little voice is given to the users of logistics such as retail companies or exporters of manufactured and time-sensitive goods who actually suffer from the supply-chain inefficiencies.

The situation is exacerbated by a lack of skills and a limited culture of supply-chain management among private and public sector managers. A limited presence of international logistics companies implies a limited exposure to international best practices in the field of supply-chain management. The region is one of the most isolated from international logistics knowledge. As proposed below, a greater involvement of global logistics operators in order to facilitate long-distance transit would lead to greater spillovers in the region.

Since the late 1990s, the region has seen a series of initiatives attempting to address some of these trade and transport facilitation issues. These initiatives have created a more-or-less institutionalized framework governed by a secretariat, such as as the Central Asia Regional Economic Cooperation (CAREC) as a sponsoring organization or the Transport Corridor Europe-Caucasus-Asia (TRACECA). These initiatives,[2] especially CAREC, have played and are still playing an important role in raising awareness and helping address local bottlenecks on certain road and rail corridors. However, because of their focus on specific routes, those corridor initiatives could not address the capacity and policy constraints at the countrywide level (for example, customs or trucking reforms), nor could they substitute for deeper regional harmonization and integration of cross-border or transit logistics, as has been done in integrated regions such as the European Union (EU) or the Association of Southeast Asian Nations, for instance. Unfortunately the complexity of regional politics challenges the implementation of deeper cross-border integration in trade and transportation within the corridor initiatives.

## Drivers for Change

Two recent developments are likely to encourage significant changes, both to the institutions that facilitate trade and to the private sector, in the way that it operates and establishes trade and transport connections in the region. First is the implementation of the Eurasian Customs Union, which includes Belarus, Kazakhstan, and Russia. It posits a very high degree of integration of rules and procedures, compared with earlier initiatives. Since customs control between borders of the Union members has been phased out, the Customs Union has a direct facilitation impact. Reportedly it also helped simplify trade with the non-Union countries because the Customs Union member countries share a single transit system for goods flowing through their territory.

The Customs Union also facilitates the integration of transport services (such as railways) and improves the possibilities for trucks to operate across borders. According to an interview with the private sector, the Union seems to have had a positive impact on supply-chain connectivity in Central Asia since coming into force in 2012. Irrespective of who may join it, the Union is likely to provide a common "acquis," in the EU sense, for trade and transport facilitation in Central Asia.[3]

The second major development is the strong interest of the government of China to develop and facilitate overland trade with the region, as a part of the country's strategy to further develop its western provinces: Major rail infrastructure is being completed to increase the capacity toward Kazakhstan and the Kyrgyz Republic. Special zones are being created at borders such as Khorgos (Xinjiang Province in China and Kazakhstan). China is also supporting the

**Table O.1  How the Measures in the Plan of Action Will Affect Supply-Chain Performance against the Six Dimensions of the Logistics Performance Index**

| Dimensions in logistics performance | Relevance for countries in the Central Asia region | Quality of trade and transport-related infrastructure | Efficiency of customs (border) clearance process | Competence and quality of logistics services | Ease of arranging competitively priced international shipments | Ability to track and trace consignments | Timeliness |
|---|---|---|---|---|---|---|---|
| Infrastructure assets | All | ● | ◑ | ◔ | ○ | ◔ | ◑ |
| Moving containers | All, in particular Kazakhstan and Uzbekistan | ◑ | ◑ | ◕ | ◕ | ● | ● |
| Regulation of logistics services | All | ○ | ◔ | ● | ● | ◑ | ◕ |
| Trade and transit facilitation | All, in particular Kazakhstan and Uzbekistan | ○ | ● | ◑ | ◕ | ◕ | ◕ |

*Source:* World Bank data.

*Note:* ○ = no impact, ◔ = limited impact, ◑ = some impact, ◕ = significant impact, ● = most impact.

development of infrastructure in the Kyrgyz Republic and Tajikistan. This policy already shows a gradual reorientation of trade of the Eastern former Soviet Union countries (Kazakhstan and the Kyrgyz Republic) toward China. The main political arm of this policy is the Shanghai Cooperation Organization, which includes Central Asian republics, except Turkmenistan, and Russia.

## Measures to Improve Connectivity

Four broad sets of measures have to be implemented either nationally or across countries (table O.1). Unlike the current corridor approach, they are not corridor-specific. They will increase the handling capacity and reliability of land transport routes, while reducing transportation costs and lead times.

## Improving the Quality of Transport Links and Cross-Border Connectivity

Programs and support toward the planning and budgeting of road maintenance of the recently rehabilitated and to some extent upgraded assets will have to be increased to ensure proper maintenance of the new assets. Technical assistance is ongoing in most countries (Kazakhstan, the Kyrgyz Republic, Tajikistan, and Uzbekistan) for the introduction of road asset management systems that should introduce efficient programming, planning, and budgeting of maintenance. Sufficient financing for maintenance has to be allocated by the respective governments. At the same time, most governments in the region are pursuing the development of new road and rail links to further develop and integrate their road and rail networks at the national and regional levels. Those investments include, for example, the Zhezkazgan-Beineu rail link (Kazakhstan), the Angren-Pap rail link (Uzbekistan), and the North-South and East-West link (the Kyrgyz Republic). Economic evaluation should determine the attractiveness and rationale for those new links, in particular their strategic importance for the development of an integrated rail and road network at the regional level with facilitation of cross-border connectivity. Substantial progress has been achieved in raising the quality of transportation links in the region, which has had substantial impacts on the movement of freight and goods. However, new projects need to assess the cost-effectiveness of investments and analyze specific the impact on improving Eurasian connections. Three measures can be identified:

- *Improve existing road and railway links* along the east-west and north-south axis to be able to efficiently address transportation demand and present the status of ongoing rehabilitation and upgrades at regional forums such as CAREC.

- *Focus on adequate maintenance policies and financing:* This implies detailed analysis of the maintenance needs and requirements in the future at the national level, an introduction of planning tools, and a firm commitment by the governments to adequate financing. The introduction of private companies to operate and maintain assets could be considered if the current pilots are shown to be successful.

- *Recreate cross-border road and rail links of regional importance:* With the breakup of the Soviet Union, road and rail networks disintegrated, requiring countries to focus on improving internal communications within each new state rather than strengthening the regional network. Similarly, pursuing the interest of developing transit potential involves elements of competition because each country has proclaimed it would prefer as much transit as possible to go through its territory. Although diversification of transport routes is a natural process in the search for means to reduce transport costs, it has resulted in a nonconducive environment that has often neglected road and rail links of regional importance. The connections in the Ferghana Valley are one example in this respect.

## Moving Containers Efficiently: Europe and East Asia Rail Freight

Most rail transit going through the borders of Kazakhstan with China or Russia terminates inland in Kazakhstan or serves other Central Asian countries. The share of China-Russia-Europe transit traffic is still a very small part of the total freight bound for the region, in spite of serious efforts to develop it. Both Central Asian and Europe-Asia logistics face the same problems of efficiency and fragmentation of the transit supply chain. One issue is the lack of continuity of rail transit traceability between China and the Customs Union, which contributes to the inability to trace transported freight and containers from their origin to the transloading facility at the border. Another problem is the apparent lack of reliable schedules for container and freight wagons, which is an operational problem, but it is compounded by the fragmentation of small-scale terminal facilities. This means it is difficult to have reliable and scheduled services for both regional and Eurasian transit.

Much remains to be done in Kazakhstan, which is pivotal for both Euro-Asian transit and transit to the Central Asian countries:

- *Establish or reinforce alliances with international freight forwarders and railways* in Europe, Russia, and China to promote scheduled consolidated services organized by international freight forwarders or railways both through and to Central Asia. This may include expanding scheduling of container block trains to selected priority terminals in Central Asian countries, other than Kazakhstan (for example, Uzbekistan).

- *Consolidate scheduled trains on fewer terminals:* This implies a discussion with railway companies and private terminal owners to determine the optimal destination of block trains in Kazakhstan and eventually other Central Asian destination countries. It may imply the planning of a larger terminal (with a capacity of 100,000 TEU or more).

- *Establish a continuous "track and trace" system for transit merchandise:* This is mostly the responsibility of international freight forwarders; a better protocol on exchange of information should be set up to facilitate transit, notably at the Customs Union border, between operators and trading companies, Customs (starting with Kazakhstan), and international freight forwarders.

## Enhancing the Private Sector in Logistics Services

The logistics industry in Central Asia is not very well developed or integrated with the global logistics industry. Freight forwarders, third-party logistics providers, and customs brokers are essentially local companies with no international linkages and a limited range of provided services. Forwarders typically operate under contracts with the railways with which they act like agents: they have no exclusive connections with international logistics companies. Such a poor state of the logistics industry serves as a major constraint to developing the role of Central Asia as a land bridge, as well as a major source of fragmentation of supply chains going through the regions of China, Kazakhstan, and Russia. It is a barrier to partnerships with international companies that can help connect the countries along the Silk Route.

Domestic trucking has no regulation of entry or distinction between commercial trucking and own-account activities. Such a distinction exists in most countries in the world and serves as a base for better sector competition, as well as a precondition for sound sector development. In Central Asia, it is only the small segment of international Transports Internationaux Routiers (TIR) trucking that has very well defined industry standards due to the need to comply with the TIR system.

The main regulatory areas include the following:

- *Establish professional standards for domestic truckers* consistent with international standards and separate commercial activities from own-account transportation. This could be done through technical assistance targeted toward conversion of all operators to those standards.
- *Define the role of freight forwarders* according to international standards and not just as a commercial agent to the railway companies; the status of transport intermediaries in some countries (such as Tajikistan) should be clarified accordingly.
- *Align the regulation of customs brokers* with international best practices.

## Expanding Trade and Transit Facilitation Initiatives

At the moment, the trade facilitation framework is still in transition, with compliance with international best practices and encouragement of compliant private operators still underdeveloped. As a result, the organization of the customs clearance process has only partially moved away from the legacy systems of bonded warehouses; paper documentation; and de facto, quasi-indispensable, intervention of customs brokers.

Another feature is the role of transit, because most import goods for consumption are not cleared at the border but almost entirely at inland destinations, near the economic centers. The Customs Union transit regime is applied in a way that seems to deviate from international practices (it is more complex with less freedom for compliant transit operators); Kazakhstan plays a pivotal role in transit transportation to the region because of its geographic location.

Supply chains also suffer from restrictions to the movement of trucks or transit. Through the system of bilateral permits, countries apply restrictions for non-TIR trucks.

Five subareas in trade facilitation should be targeted as priorities:

- *Move to paperless customs declaration and reinforce customs capacity*, allowing at least regular traders to submit their customs declarations online, without the intervention of customs brokers. Capacity of customs in particular in the area of risk management is particularly warranted.

- *Facilitate the development of authorized economic operators and traders:* It might be difficult to implement the authorized trader regime on a regional basis, but it should be encouraged on a country basis, at least in the large economies. Existing requirements may be streamlined without creating fiscal risk or deviating from international best practices (for instance, ownership of facilities, submission deadlines, and auditing procedures), in particular in Kazakhstan and Uzbekistan.

- *Improve the implementation of the Customs Union transit regime in Russia and Kazakhstan*, which in practice means proposing solutions to align the internal Customs Union transit implementation mechanism with the EU common transit. This component does not require special discussions with the private sector but implies consultations with experts on European common transit. The compatibility of the TIR, a problem that has surfaced recently, is also to be addressed.

- *Facilitate transit and cross-border trade through interconnections of the transit information systems in the regional countries:* The countries in the region have computerized trade systems. Protocols of exchange of information would help facilitate transit and manage cross-border trade. For instance, for the importing country, the ability to access information on exporters from the neighboring country would allow facilitating implementation of rules of origin and control fraud and smuggling. This should be implemented in priority between countries in the Customs Union.

- *Phase out existing obstacles to transit by trucks*, including (1) the restrictive list of products allowed for transit and (2) restriction of passage of non-TIR trucks from a country in the region. This would include the consolidation of existing bilateral agreements on permits with China, so that trucks originating anywhere within Central Asia can pick up deliveries at the border and transit through third countries.

## Notes

1. Republic of Kazakhstan (Kazakhstan), Kyrgyz Republic, Republic of Tajikistan (Tajikistan), Republic of Turkmenistan (Turkmenistan), and Republic of Uzbekistan (Uzbekistan).
2. See appendix A for a list of initiatives.
3. Whether the Customs Union should include other Central Asian countries, other than Kazakhstan, is beyond the scope of this work because in addition to logistics there are other dimensions (fiscal, trade policy, and so on). The Kyrgyz Republic and Tajikistan have expressed interest.

## Reference

World Bank. 2007. *Connecting to Compete: Trade Logistics in the Global Economy.* World Bank, Washington, DC.

# CHAPTER 1

# From the Old to the Modern Silk Route

The Silk Route and the role of Central Asia as a land bridge between Europe and China has been a resurgent one throughout history.[1] Today the potential exists to re-create transit trade through this route. However, the main flows and the main challenges will be establishing reliable supply chains that will sustain the landlocked economies in Central Asia and connect them to the main markets in the west and the east. This objective requires not only investment in physical infrastructure but also measures to reduce trade costs and supply fragmentation across borders. Connectivity improvements will facilitate regional trade, long-distance trade to Europe and China, and will also participate in boosting the transit potential on the modern Silk Route.

## Looking Back at the Old Silk Road

A hundred years ago, Sir Halford Mackinder, the founder of the discipline of "geopolitics," described the Central Asia region as the "geographical pivot of history" to characterize its role in not only bridging but also influencing the destiny of Europe and East Asia, and to give tribute to the fascination it has attracted for centuries. Indeed, the Eurasian link through Central Asia, known as the Silk Route or Silk Road, represents the oldest recorded transcontinental trade flow of great historical importance. It is also mentioned or described by many commentators since antiquity, from Strabo and Pliny the Elder through Marco Polo.

Trade between Europe and East Asia, especially China, was active from the end of the Roman Empire until the end of the Middle Ages and consisted mostly of the import of silk, for which China maintained a strong comparative advantage over a long period despite the fact that the production process from the secretions of the silkworm or *Bombyx mori* had already been identified by Pliny. The land route went through Asia Minor and Persia, Bactria (currently Uzbekistan), and then all the way to Xi'an in China.

Interestingly, the old Silk Road shares many common features with the modern Silk Route or land transport connection between Europe and Asia through Central Asia. In this report it is called the "Eurasian Connection."

First, as observed by Pliny (*"imperii nostri exhauriente India et merces remittente, quae apud nos centiplicato veneant"*), trade was highly unbalanced in favor of China, implying a flow of precious metals from west to east, a matter of concern for imperial authorities, who, at times, restricted imports. Second, this land transport route has been for long periods in competition with a maritime route, or, in modern language, a "multimodal transportation route." From the time the Romans controlled Egypt, reliable sea links to India were established to allow Chinese silk to transit by a shorter land route (through the Indus or Ganges valleys), leading to lower costs and higher volumes.

Obviously then, as now, the merits of the northern land bridge as compared with the southern maritime route depended upon the political willingness of the countries of transit to facilitate trade toward Europe. The Parthians, and then the Arabs and the Turks, enjoyed long periods of domination over the first 15 centuries of the modern era, when they could control and eventually stop the commercial access of European nations into China. Since the sixteenth century the fast development of direct maritime trade between Europe and East Asia made the land bridge irrelevant.

## The Eurasian Connection Nowadays

Today the shipping route through the Suez Canal supports most Euro-Asia trade with a throughput of 40 million twenty-foot equivalent units for containers and 500 million tons of bulk merchandise. Nonetheless, the rail link between China and Europe is currently enjoying renewed interest because it may offer competitive trade-offs in costs and delays over the maritime route. Several multinational companies are already operating regular container "block" trains on this route through Kazakhstan and the Russian Federation. But the land bridge is currently not and likely never will be competitive in terms of volume, because its potential throughput is only a small fraction (about 1–2 percent) of what is currently carried by sea. It may, however, become the adequate and alternative solution for a few time-sensitive supply chains involving manufacturing production sharing, such as for high-value components in the automotive or computer industries.

Even more than the transit business opportunity, the trade and transport linkages are also essential to sustain regional economies in the Central Asian republics, not only because of their dependence on Europe and China for trade in Asian imports and exports but also to promote local added value and trade opportunities between themselves, as in ancient times. The modern Central Asia region comprises five independent republics: Kazakhstan, the Kyrgyz Republic, Tajikistan, Turkmenistan, and Uzbekistan. These countries together have a population of about 40 million. Russian Siberia and the province of Xinjiang in western China, which are also part of the modern Silk Route, account for about 20 million each.

The Eurasian Connection • http://dx.doi.org/10.1596/978-0-8213-9912-5

The long-distance trade of the republics of Central Asia consists entirely of energy and mineral products, but regional trade—although small—is more diversified, because the distance from main suppliers makes local value added viable in many activities. For instance, the region has several car assembly plants, such as General Motors in Uzbekistan, and the ArcelorMittal pipe-manufacturing plant in Kazakhstan. Facilitating regional trade on the modern Silk Route is important to create linkages and opportunities between Central Asia, western China, and eastern Russia.

What makes a trade route today is not just the physical infrastructure or a path on a map, but the actual supply chains that run through various links connecting importers to exporters. In a functional sense, more than the radical change in transportation technology since the Middle Ages, the integration of supply chains is what differentiates the modern ("new") Silk Route from the old one, which depended on a fragmented caravan trade. There was no direct business connection between buyers and sellers, and trade happened through a long, and costly, series of transactions in the famous trading cities along the route. Today, in the context of development, fragmentation still exists, creating weak links and reducing the efficiency of supply chains. Intrusive border controls, reliance on local intermediaries such as brokers, unreliable transport services by rail or road, and weak infrastructure make supply chains more fragmented in the sense that the principal (shipper or global logistics company) does not have full control of what happens in transit.

## The Silk Route Countries: Trade and Physical Networks

The five Central Asian republics have relatively unique geographical, human, and economic features that shape their trade and development and also make transportation and logistics especially critical to their economic potential. They are in the heart of the largest landmass, Eurasia. Distances between the main trading partners in China, Russia, and Europe are very great. Economic activities, and the potential for diversification, are constrained by a low average population density, and regional supply chains are extended over long distances. The typical length of intraregional corridors is in the same range as the typical transport route on the African continent (1,000–2,000 kilometers [km]), which many development experts consider a major constraint to trade.

Another illustration of this density challenge is that the total population of Central Asian countries is almost exactly that of France, about 65 million inhabitants (as of 2012). However, they are spread over seven times as great an area (4 million km², about the same size as the entire land area of the EU) and have a GDP of about one-tenth that of France. Furthermore, production locations and population accumulation are relatively unevenly distributed. The population density is much higher (table 1.1) in the southern part of the region (foremost in the Ferghana Valley of Uzbekistan).

The five Central Asian republics along the Silk Route are relatively small economies that lack an agglomeration effect because of their low population

**Table 1.1  Main Indicators for Central Asian Countries, 2012**

|  | Population (millions) | Surface area (1,000 km²) | Density (inhabitants/km²) | GDP per capita ($, 2011) |
|---|---|---|---|---|
| Kazakhstan | 16.6 | 2,725 | 6 | 11,357 |
| Kyrgyz Republic | 5.5 | 200 | 28 | 1,075 |
| Tajikistan | 7.0 | 143 | 49 | 935 |
| Turkmenistan | 5.1 | 488 | 10 | 5,497 |
| Uzbekistan | 29.3 | 447 | 66 | 1,546 |
| Central Asia | 63.5 | 4,003 | 16 | 4,314 |

*Source:* World Development Indicators 2012.

**Figure 1.1  Central Asian Countries: Trade Growth as a Percentage of GDP, 2001–11**

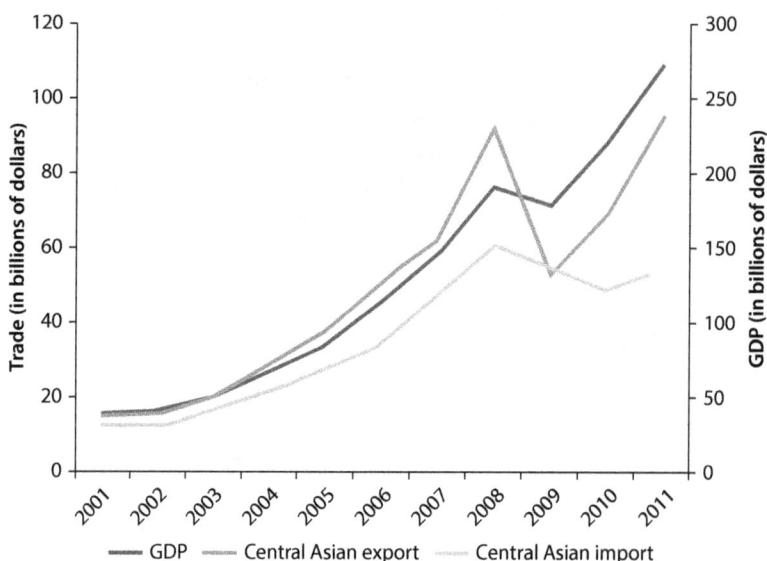

*Sources:* IMF Direction of Trade Statistics; and World Bank, World Development Indicators.

density, and thus they are inevitably dependent on imports for consumption. They have very large amounts of natural resources, primarily oil and gas, but also coal (mainly used for steel production) and mineral resources. However, these resources are not equally distributed among the five republics, leading to inequalities in development and wealth. More than two-thirds of the economic output in production in Central Asia is concentrated in Kazakhstan, which is the largest country in size, has the highest concentration of natural resources, and is—measured per capita—the most well-off country in the region. The structure of the economies is greatly biased toward heavy industries and extractive activities (40 percent of GDP on average). The share of agriculture is high in the smaller economies (the Kyrgyz Republic and Tajikistan) (figure 1.1).

Growth has been brisk (table 1.2), yet uneven, during the first decade of the twenty-first century, driven by commodity prices and demand from large markets in Europe and China. In fact, the pace of trade has not been faster than that of the growth of the economy, unlike in emerging economies where participation in international supply chains and production sharing mean that trade typically grows faster than the value added.

The materialization of the region's growth potential and the integration of the Silk Route countries depend on external and internal connectivity of the main cities in the region as well as with the rest of the world. Inherited from pre-Soviet and Soviet times, the transport infrastructure network of the Central Asian region is relatively well extended. It is situated along several international road and railway routes. These routes linking Central Asia to Europe and Asia have been studied in great detail over the last two decades, and various institutional arrangements exist to oversee them (see appendix A). Most of the routes cross one or more countries in Central Asia. As shown in table 1.3 and maps 1.1 and 1.2, Kazakhstan and Uzbekistan have the largest road and rail networks in the region. Several rail connections link the Kyrgyz Republic and Tajikistan, which are branches or end lines of the network of the former Soviet Union (map 1.2).

The goal of developing transit potential through countries' respective territories and reducing transportation costs has translated into specific plans and projects that aim to develop international transport routes as well as links within each country (map 1.3). Specific projects include constructing new and rehabilitating existing national roads and railways, improving technical facilities, and establishing logistics centers. An analysis of the official documents, such as

**Table 1.2  Central Asia and Its Peers: Production and Growth Patterns, 2010**

|  | Agriculture, % value added | Industry, % value added | Trade, % GDP | GDP growth, 10-year average |
|---|---|---|---|---|
| Kazakhstan | 6 | 40 | 67 | 7.7 |
| Kyrgyz Republic | 20 | 29 | 105 | 4.2 |
| Tajikistan | 20 | 20 | 68 | 8.5 |
| Turkmenistan | 15 | 48 | 65 | 8.8 |
| Uzbekistan | 19 | 36 | 51 | 7.4 |
| Central Asia Region | 10 | 39 | 65 | 7.3 |
| China | 10 | 47 | 50 | 10.6 |
| Germany | 1 | 28 | 76 | 1.2 |
| Russian Federation | 4 | 37 | 45 | 4.8 |

*Source:* World Development Indicators 2012.

**Table 1.3  Road and Rail Network Length in Central Asia, 2010/11**
*Thousand km*

|  | Kazakhstan | Kyrgyz Republic | Tajikistan | Turkmenistan | Uzbekistan |
|---|---|---|---|---|---|
| Rail | 14.9 | 0.45 | 0.67 | 2.44 | 4.4 |
| Road | 97.2 | 18.8 | 13.9 | 22.0 | 42.7 |

*Sources:* Agencies of Statistics, UNECE, CAREC, IRU, various sources.

**Map 1.1  Regional Road Network in Central Asia, 2012**

**Map 1.2  Regional Rail Network in Central Asia, 2012**

**Map 1.3  Long-Distance Traffic Routes through Central Asia**

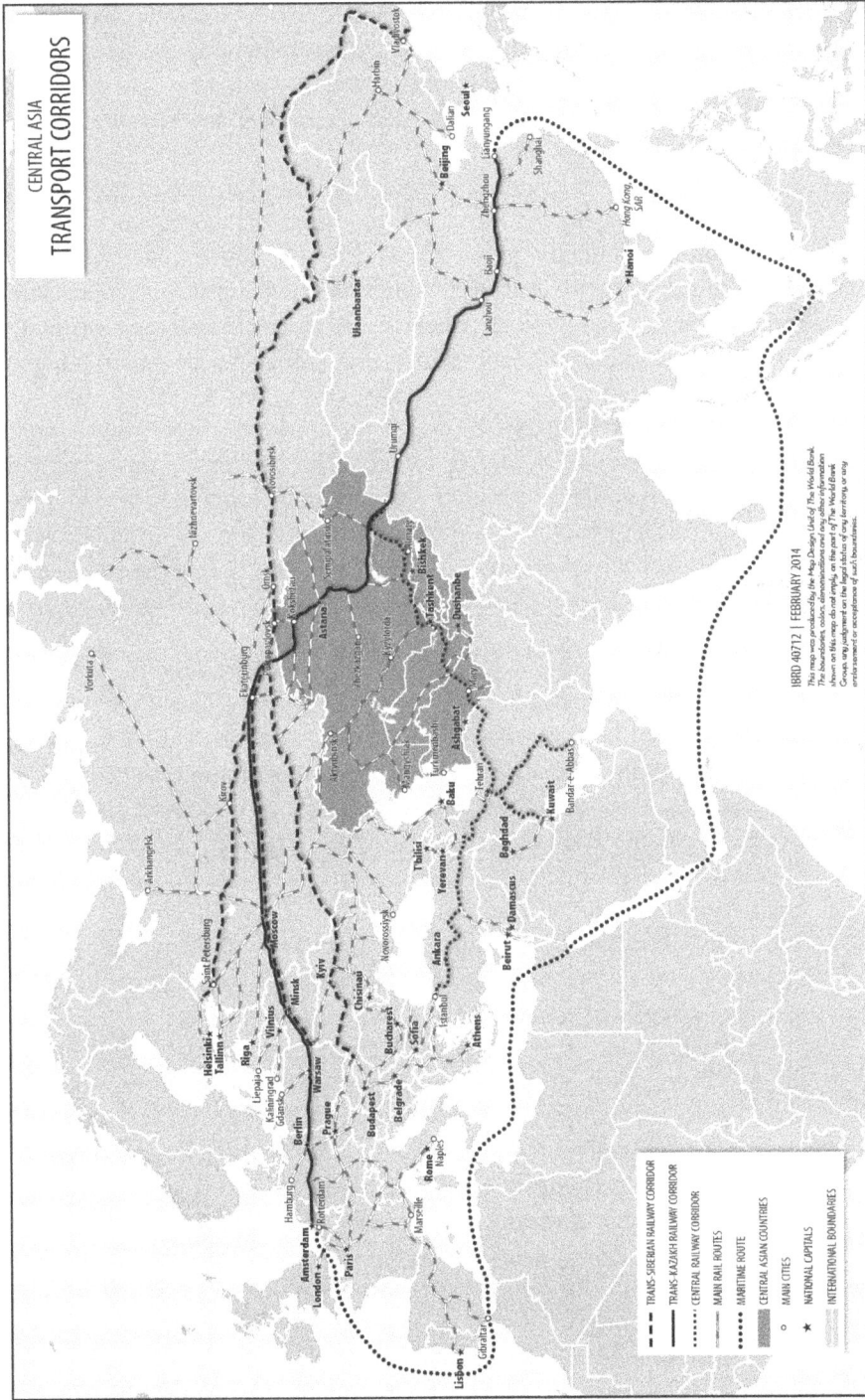

CENTRAL ASIA
TRANSPORT CORRIDORS

IBRD 40712 | FEBRUARY 2014

This map was produced by the Map Design Unit of The World Bank. The boundaries, colors, denominations and any other information shown on this map do not imply, on the part of The World Bank Group, any judgment on the legal status of any territory, or any endorsement or acceptance of such boundaries.

TRANS-SIBERIAN RAILWAY CORRIDOR
TRANS-KAZAKH RAILWAY CORRIDOR
CENTRAL RAILWAY CORRIDOR
MAIN RAIL ROUTES
MARITIME ROUTE
CENTRAL ASIAN COUNTRIES
MAIN CITIES
NATIONAL CAPITALS
INTERNATIONAL BOUNDARIES

governments' development strategies[2] and underlying transport programs[3] in Central Asia, suggests that the governments have set the development of physical connections as a clear priority. Governments of the countries have invested in transport infrastructure with support from international financial institutions. Physical investments for the rehabilitation and upgrading of the six Central Asia Regional Economic Cooperation (CAREC) corridors, for example, accounted for $1.27 billion in 2010 alone.

For Kazakhstan, the priority is the further development of the routes to and from the Chinese border (east-west axis) and the north-south axis through Turkmenistan continuing to the Islamic Republic of Iran. The most prominent example is the upgrade and rehabilitation of road transport infrastructure along the Western Europe–Western China transport corridor as well as the development of the north-south transnational rail link along the eastern shore of the Caspian Sea from Uzen (western Kazakhstan) via Gyzylgaya-Bereket-Etrek (Turkmenistan), which ends in Gorgan in the Islamic Republic of Iran. Apart from the reconstruction of rail and road infrastructure, the government of Kazakhstan has also announced its objective of developing its transport facilities to attract transit transportation through its territory, by establishing international logistics centers for intermodal freight transport. The project that receives particular attention is the construction of the ICBC at Khorgos, at the border with China.

Because of its heavy dependence on road transportation, the government of the Kyrgyz Republic is mainly focusing on the development of the country's six strategic road corridors along the north-south as well as east-west axes. Most recently, the Ministry of Transport and Communications of the Kyrgyz Republic has proposed the reconstruction of a second north-south link as an alternative to the Bishkek-Osh road. Additionally, the government has been discussing several options to expand its relatively small rail network of 450 km, which consists of end lines of the rail network of the former Soviet Union. The proposed east-west and north-south rail links, albeit requiring substantial investments, would establish an integrated rail network that could move some of the freight off the road.

Although Tajikistan set a goal of promoting international freight transit through its territory, its own transit options are heavily constrained by a strong dependence on the Kyrgyz Republic and Uzbekistan for transit traffic. The government is therefore focusing on developing additional transport connections by rehabilitating and upgrading road transport links to Afghanistan, China, and the Kyrgyz Republic through several outlets. Additionally, development of a new railway link is being discussed, linking the territory of Tajikistan with Afghanistan and Turkmenistan, for which a memorandum has been signed by the three participating countries.

With an estimated 22,000 km of roads and 2,440 km of railroad lines, the government of Turkmenistan announced its intention to redouble its efforts to integrate its highway and railroad systems more closely with continental east-west routes across the Islamic Republic of Iran and to begin by upgrading its main road and rail links to both Afghanistan and the Islamic Republic of Iran.

Uzbekistan's focus is exclusively on the development of international transport routes with an investment plan of more than $6.9 billion, mainly along the north-south axis for rail development with connection to Afghanistan as well as along the A380 highway connecting Uzbekistan with Afghanistan, Kazakhstan, the Kyrgyz Republic, Tajikistan, and Turkmenistan. The construction of a new rail link from Angren to Pap to connect the rail network of the Ferghana Valley with the rest of the country began in late 2013.

The development of new rail and road links is also being considered to offer better ongoing service in meeting intraregional and transcontinental trade demand and providing alternative routes. However, transit volumes have fallen far below those achieved during the Soviet era. Nevertheless, Kazakhstan continues to occupy a central position as a transit country for the region. Imbalances in trade patterns of the economies have significant implications for flows along transport routes. The imbalances make efficient operations in both modes very difficult, because little opportunity exists for backhaul freight.

## Establishing Reliable Supply Chains

Establishing a sustainable supply chain and reliable trade and transportation connections is not just a matter of private demand, but is largely dependent on country factors such as infrastructure, services, or customs captured in the concept of logistics performance. Policy does affect national logistics performance. This outcome depends on government intervention in areas such as infrastructure regulation and focuses on services or customs border management and trade facilitation. Cross-border cooperation to harmonize logistics regulations and facilitate international supply chains is also essential, especially for landlocked countries such as those in Central Asia, which depend on each other to trade globally.

In Central Asia, most physical links for regional and international trade are essentially available for trains and trucks. The breakup of the former Soviet Union left its member countries with the task of reconstructing seamless logistics systems across borders and over long distances to trade between themselves and with their eastern and western partners. The new supply chain, unlike those in the earlier systems, builds upon the delivery of logistics services according to market principles and modern trade- and transport-related institutions.

Evidence shows that this transition is still not complete in Central Asia, because the countries experience high trade costs and comparatively low logistics performance. Field surveys point to low reliability of regional supply chains and to inevitably high costs and border and transit delays. The quality of services is marred by operational constraints and fragmented local markets. Given their common history, countries share many similar institutional challenges in improving their connectivity.

The Eurasian Connection • http://dx.doi.org/10.1596/978-0-8213-9912-5

## Notes

1. The reference is comparatively recent. It was coined by Ferdinand von Richthofen, a German scholar and explorer at the end of the nineteenth century. The original German word "Seidenstraße" is translated indifferently as Silk Road or Route (as in this document) and seldom as Silk Way.

2. Current development strategies include Kazakhstan 2030; Kyrgyz Republic National Strategy for Sustainable Development 2013–17; National Development Strategy of the Republic of Tajikistan for the period to 2015; Strategy of Economic, Political and Cultural Development of Turkmenistan up to 2020; and Uzbekistan 2030.

3. Current transport plans and strategies include Transport Strategy of the Republic of Kazakhstan 2007–15; Kyrgyz Republic Transport Sector Master Plan; Tajikistan Transport Sector Master Plan; and Development of Infrastructure, Transport and Communication Construction 2011–15 in the Republic of Uzbekistan.

## Reference

World Bank. 2012. *World Development Indicators*. Washington, DC: World Bank.

# CHAPTER 2

# Connecting Central Asia to the World

Central Asian countries trade mostly with Western Europe, China, and the Russian Federation. Their exports are concentrated in raw materials and energy, as is discussed in the first section of this chapter. Regional trade remains small, and hence Central Asian countries are very dependent on import supply chains by train and truck over very long distances from Europe and Asia.[1]

Supply chains with countries outside the region connect the five countries on the modern Silk Route to Europe and China, through Turkey, Russia, or other Central Asian countries. Mostly these supply chains serve the import needs of Silk Route countries; increasingly they also support a small but growing Euro-Asian (transcontinental) transit trade. The potential of long-distance connections as well as regional connections is the subject of the following two chapters.

How these connections serve the regions depends not only on the actual routes and services but also on the domestic capability to connect to these routes and services, captured in the concept of logistics performance. Logistics performance, discussed in the third section, depends on various factors, most of them dependent on the implementation of policies in areas such as customs, infrastructure, or private services. Although Central Asian countries are geographically located between the two most logistically efficient regions in the world, they face serious logistics bottlenecks, which, combined with those imposed by geography, result in high trade costs between the region and the rest of the world, as discussed in the second section.

Furthermore, existing patterns of logistics are still very influenced by the legacy of the former Soviet Union (FSU), which means that the smaller countries located farther away from the main Eurasian routes through Kazakhstan and Russia face even more daunting connectivity challenges. The fourth section provides a snapshot of new trends and opportunities arising with the emergence of trade from western China, on the one hand, and the Eurasian Customs Union, on the other, which both provide opportunities for reduced costs and increased trade for the countries along the modern Silk Route.

## Pattern of Trade along the Modern Silk Route

Trade in the Central Asia region is very asymmetric. Exports are dominated by commodities, with Kazakhstan being the main exporter (over 85 percent). Import patterns are more balanced between countries, because the import basket is more diversified. One of the main features of imports is its reorientation toward China at the expense of Russia and other regions, except for Western Europe, which remains a strong trade partner of Central Asia. The growth rate of trade with China (table 2.1) has been twice as fast in Central Asia compared with the rest of the world (40 percent per year over 2001–10 as compared with 20 percent elsewhere).

The main extra-regional exports from the southern part of the region are mineral commodities, steel, and cotton. Regional trade is relatively small, representing only a few percent of the total trade of Central Asia. However, it is very important for the Kyrgyz Republic and Uzbekistan. The basket of products is more diversified than for extra-regional exports (table 2.2).

Oil producers such as Kazakhstan sell to their neighbors and in return buy food products (fruit and vegetables, notably from the Kyrgyz Republic). The trade in manufactures is limited (table 2.3), and the proximity of Chinese

### Table 2.1  Change in Origins of Imports for Central Asian Countries: Emergence of China, 2000–10

*Percent*

|                    | 2000 | 2010 |
|--------------------|------|------|
| Central Asia       | 9.5  | 6.8  |
| China              | 2.4  | 20.5 |
| Russian Federation | 29.4 | 18.9 |
| European Union     | 19.4 | 19.5 |
| *(Germany)*        | *5.9* | *5.5* |
| Turkey             | 2.6  | 2.3  |
| World              | 100  | 100  |

*Source:* IMF Direction of Trade Statistics (import statistics).

### Table 2.2  Share of Regional Trade among Central Asian Countries

*Percent*

| Country | Share in Central Asia exports | Share in Central Asia imports | Share of GDP | Share of Central Asia in country imports | Share of Central Asia in country exports |
|---------|-------------------------------|-------------------------------|--------------|------------------------------------------|------------------------------------------|
| Kazakhstan      | 83.9 | 49.2 | 68.7 | 2.8  | 3.6  |
| Kyrgyz Republic | 1.5  | 14.8 | 2.2  | 9.0  | 44.9 |
| Tajikistan      | 1.8  | 5.4  | 2.4  | 17.5 | 2.9  |
| Turkmenistan    | 4.7  | 11.6 | 10.2 | 4.3  | 4.0  |
| Uzbekistan      | 8.1  | 19.0 | 16.6 | 16.6 | 15.4 |
| Central Asia    |      |      |      | 7.3  | 5.2  |

*Source:* IMF Direction of Trade Statistics (import statistics).

**Table 2.3  Matrix of Regional Trade, 2010**
*Millions $*

| Country | Kazakhstan | Kyrgyz Republic | Tajikistan | Turkmenistan | Uzbekistan | Total |
|---|---|---|---|---|---|---|
| Kazakhstan | 0.0 | 165.7 | 16.6 | 9.5 | 473.3 | 665.2 |
| Kyrgyz Republic | 466.7 | 0.0 | 7.5 | 2.5 | 177.9 | 654.6 |
| Tajikistan | 292.7 | 15.4 | 0.0 | 83.5 | 71.8 | 463.4 |
| Turkmenistan | 100.7 | 5.2 | 1.4 | 0.0 | 134.0 | 241.3 |
| Uzbekistan | 1,211.3 | 283.7 | 9.5 | 34.7 | 0.0 | 1,539.2 |
| Total | 2,071.4 | 470.0 | 35.0 | 130.2 | 857.0 | 3,563.6 |

*Source:* IMF Direction of Trade Statistics (import statistics).

industry makes the development of labor-intensive manufacturing challenging. Nonetheless, some examples are encouraging, such as in the automotive sector, where there appear to be some advantages in assembling near consumer markets. Several manufacturers—the biggest plant is General Motors in Uzbekistan, and notably some of Toyota's investments in Kazakhstan—appear to take advantage of the central location between Europe and Asia to bring parts from both regions for assembly in Central Asia (box 2.1).

However, diversification and volumes of regional trade in Central Asia remain limited when compared with those in other developing regions, even with groups of countries that have apparent similarities with the region, because they have not transitioned toward manufacturing (as is the case of the Association of Southeast Asian Nations). In comparison, the countries of Central America trade 18 percent between themselves, about three times more than Central Asia (table 2.2). Countries in the francophone monetary union (UEMOA) in West Africa also trade at the same level, although all of them are poorer than Central Asia. In these cases the lack of diversification of exports toward the main rich partners (commodities in both cases) does not prevent the emergence of significant trade in local products such as food, construction material, and light manufactures.

The intraregional distances may challenge trade integration and the emergence of regional supply chains. However, limited regional trade highlights supply-side challenges and trade and transport facilitation bottlenecks that result from limited regional integration. For example, Central America as well as Africa has engaged for several decades in a regional integration policy, resulting in free trade zones and economic unions, which so far have not emerged in Central Asia since the breakup of the FSU.

## Trade Costs Patterns along the Modern Silk Route

The concept of trade costs (box 2.2) provides an effective way to describe quantitatively the trade connectivity patterns of Central Asian countries with Europe and Asia as well as among themselves. The intensity of trade between countries is reduced by many factors that capture the degree of separation between them

## Box 2.1  General Motors Uzbekistan

The automotive sector in Uzbekistan produces passenger vehicles, light commercial vehicles, and heavy trucks. The three original equipment manufacturers are General Motors (GM) Uzbekistan, SamAuto, and Man Auto. The products of the automotive sector are sold domestically and exported to neighboring countries via the different distribution channels. Nearly all of the exports are automobiles. The principal imports are components used for the manufacture of automobiles.

When a 50/50 joint venture (introduced in 1996) between the government of Uzbekistan and Daewoo Motor Company of the Republic of Korea went bankrupt in the early 2000s, the government modernized the plant at Asaka and brought in GM as a partner to provide technical and engineering capabilities. A new company, GM Uzbekistan, was established, with GM holding a 25 percent share and JSC UzAutoProm the remainder. The principal activities of the plant are stamping, assembly, and painting.

The volume of exports, which had dropped to about 50,000 vehicles in 2009, is now about 90,000. In the fall of 2012 the company began production of the Chevrolet Cobalt, with annual production expected to reach 85,000 in 2013. Over 60 percent of production is intended for export.

For imported inputs, GM Uzbekistan continues to rely on the supply chains developed by Daewoo. Most of the suppliers are Korean, and imports from the Republic of Korea amount to about 30,000 twenty-foot equivalent units per year. Nearly all of these are shipped from Busan, unloaded in the Lianyungang port, and then transported in block trains to Angren. These trains operate twice weekly under an agreement with China Railways. Because of the reported unreliability of this route, in 2012 GM Uzbekistan established an alternative weekly service on the Trans-Siberian route from Nakhodka, even though this route is about 2,000 km longer. The shipments are arranged by international freight forwarders, whereas the movements within Uzbekistan are arranged by the Angren Logistics Center and DHL. The transit time from the unloading port to Tashkent is typically about 15 days.

Beginning with the production of the Cobalt, the inbound supply chains will be modified to utilize GM's international supply network managed by its central procurement service. Inputs from Canada, India, Mexico, Thailand, and the United States will be transshipped via Busan, whereas Brazilian and European imports will be handled through Bremen and Hamburg and shipped by rail through Russia. The inputs will be purchased either free carrier or free on board and shipped using a through bill of lading or a combined bill. The routing of cargo will be determined at the corporate level. The inputs will be delivered by rail to the logistics hub at Angren and from there transported by road to the Ferghana Valley.

Despite the efforts to increase local production, the amount of imported inputs currently consumed in Uzbekistan averages one container load forty-foot equivalent unit per six to seven cars, which accounts for most of the weight of the car. The failure to move beyond a relatively small percentage of local content is due to the limited scale of production, which discourages suppliers from investing in local production facilities. Global suppliers of standardized components concentrate production in larger clusters and ship the components from there to the smaller clusters, and thus the components will not be locally produced until sufficient demand is seen.

*Source:* World Bank 2013.

## Box 2.2 What Are the Sources of Trade Costs?

Trade costs have two main categories of sources. The first have to do with entirely bilateral factors of separation between the exporter and the importer, which are more dependent on exogenous factors rather than particular policy choices. Examples include the following:

- Geographical distance.
- Transportation costs or the delays associated with transportation and logistics.
- Common features between trading partners such as language, common history, sharing a common border, or participation in the same economic community.

The second category consists of endogenous trade costs, which are factors specific to the origin or destination, and which in a sense represent the "thickness" of borders. These sources of costs can be targeted by adequate national or regional policies in areas such as transportation, trade, or trade facilitation. Examples include the following:

- Logistics performance (cost, delay, and reliability) and bottlenecks on international supply chains (such as border control and transit systems with third countries).
- International connectivity, such as the existence of regular maritime, air, or terrestrial services, notably in view of the hub-and-spokes organization of international transportation.
- Tariffs.
- Nontariff measures.

The recently published World Bank–UNESCAP data set (Arvis et al. 2013) proposes comprehensive measures of trade costs for 178 countries over the 1995–2010 period using the inverse gravity methodology. The trade costs are ad valorem equivalents computed from trade and production data. Trade costs in this construction are symmetric. Trade costs remain high in the developing world and have not on average been going down.

and create "friction" or trade costs. Trade costs are the price equivalent of the reduction of international trade as compared with the potential implied by domestic production and consumption in the origin and destination markets. Higher bilateral trade costs result in smaller bilateral trade flows.

Distance remains the single most important source of trade costs worldwide. Given low population density and the geographic patterns of Central Asia, distance naturally functions against the development of trade supply chains in the five Central Asian republics along the Silk Route. However, research shows that factors such as the quality of logistics, trade facilitation, and the connectivity of international infrastructure explain at least as much as trade costs. These factors are all influenced by policies carried out at the national or regional level in areas of infrastructure, railways, enabling of services, or trade facilitation. In the case of Central Asia, the many sources of costs are scrutinized in the following chapters: lack of facilitation at the border, low efficiency of services, and fragmentation in supply chains. Policy makers can and should compensate for the impact

The Eurasian Connection  •  http://dx.doi.org/10.1596/978-0-8213-9912-5

of large distances and the consequences of being in landlocked locations through appropriate policy measures, although these factors can never be eliminated.

Bilateral trade costs are available[2] for two countries along the Silk Route (Kazakhstan and the Kyrgyz Republic) as well as two countries along the Eurasian land bridge (Belarus and Russia). The countries in this region have much higher trade costs with the main European and Asian partners in the region than between themselves. This is apparent when comparing the trade costs profile for regional and Eurasian economies with the three main partner economies: China, Germany, and Russia (figure 2.1). Eurasia could to some extent be called a trade costs "hill" between China and Europe. Moreover,

- Eurasian countries tend to have higher trade costs between themselves than European or Asian countries have between themselves (the smallest value is Russia-Kazakhstan at 66 percent, whereas trade costs in the EU are as low as 20 percent between neighbors) (see table 2.4).
- However, the costs within FSU, especially with Russia, are significantly lower than the costs of trade with the main partners outside the region (Europe and Asia).
- The trade costs penalty is particularly high for the smaller landlocked countries such as the Kyrgyz Republic (table 2.4).
- Trade costs with Europe (Germany) tend to be lower than with Asia (China) (figure 2.1 and table 2.4).

**Figure 2.1 Trade Costs Patterns, with China, Germany, and Russia, All Nonenergy Trade, 2009**

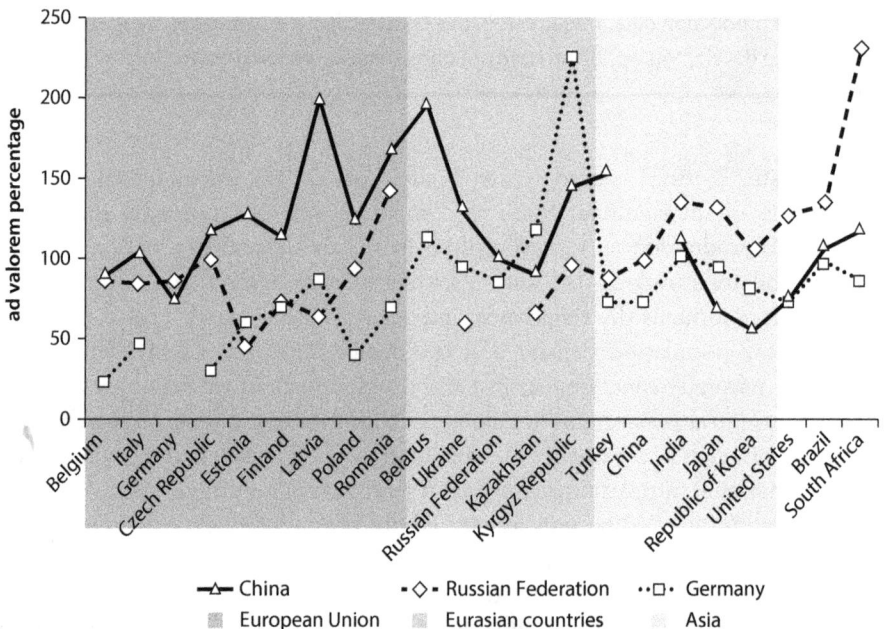

*Source:* Based on World Bank UNESCAP trade costs data set.

**Table 2.4  Eurasian Trade Costs, Nonenergy Trade, 2009 (Ad Valorem Equivalent)**
*Percentage*

|  | Belarus | Kazakhstan | Kyrgyz Republic | Russian Federation | Ukraine | Germany | China |
|---|---|---|---|---|---|---|---|
| Belarus | — | 120 | 160 | — | 66 | 113 | 196 |
| **Kazakhstan** | **120** | — | **81** | **66** | **80** | **117** | **90** |
| **Kyrgyz Republic** | **160** | **81** | — | **96** | **171** | **226** | **144** |
| Russian Federation | — | 66 | 96 | — | 60 | 86 | 99 |
| Ukraine | 66 | 80 | 171 | 60 | — | 95 | 128 |

*Note:* Bold values are data for Central Asian countries; — = not available.
*Source:* Based on World Bank UNESCAP trade costs data set.

- Eurasian countries, except for Kazakhstan and Russia, have much higher trade costs with China than the main European countries do, despite the large distance between Europe and China.

These patterns reflect several trends beyond the handicap of having to trade or transit over a very large landmass. The first is the historical orientation of the trade and logistics systems (for example, railways and main road corridors) toward Eastern and Western Europe. The increase of trade eastward is more recent. Only Kazakhstan has relatively low trade costs with China, almost comparable with its trade costs with Russia, probably reflecting the recent efforts by the government of China to promote trade across its northwestern border.

Finally, higher trade costs, especially for small countries and countries located away from the main transportation route through Russia or Kazakhstan, show that supply-chain constraints, including logistics and facilitation issues, are reducing trade in the region. We turn to this problem in the next section.

## Supply-Chain Performance in Central Asia

The efficiency of trade supply chains, or logistics performance, depends not only on infrastructure but also on the institutions and processes of trade—such as processing by customs—and the quality of services available for trade, which itself depends on regulation and competition. History has created an environment in the FSU countries that is not seen as conducive for efficient logistics and facilitation of trade. The disintegration of the Soviet Union meant that new institutions had to manage borders, and that the unified railway system became fragmented. These changes created several obstacles for further trade facilitation, which were especially detrimental to the smaller landlocked countries in Central Asia (similar to the ones in the Caucasus region) that have to trade in transit across many borders. Table 2.5 gives the most recent results of the Logistics Performance Index (see appendix B) for Central Asian countries.

The Eurasian Connection  •  http://dx.doi.org/10.1596/978-0-8213-9912-5

The most striking pattern in logistics performance in Central Asia is that the region as a whole is clearly lagging behind not only the most developed countries but also Eastern Europe, Turkey, and East Asia. Figure 2.2 compares the position of FSU countries, when adjusting for the level of development per capita. This means that the facilitation and logistics bottlenecks are indeed significant and the countries tend to lag behind in reforms.

Additionally, it could be observed that (1) the countries that have a more European orientation, such as Georgia or Ukraine, tend to do somewhat better

**Table 2.5  Logistics Performance Index Results for the Central Asian Countries, 2012**

| Country | LPI rank | LPI score | Customs | Infrastructure | International shipments | Logistics competence | Tracking and tracing | Timeliness |
|---|---|---|---|---|---|---|---|---|
| Belarus | 91 | 2.61 | 2.24 | 2.78 | 2.58 | 2.65 | 2.58 | 2.87 |
| Kazakhstan | 86 | 2.69 | 2.58 | 2.6 | 2.67 | 2.75 | 2.83 | 2.73 |
| Kyrgyz Republic | 130 | 2.35 | 2.45 | 2.49 | 2.00 | 2.25 | 2.31 | 2.69 |
| Russian Federation | 95 | 2.58 | 2.04 | 2.45 | 2.59 | 2.65 | 2.76 | 3.02 |
| Tajikistan | 136 | 2.28 | 2.43 | 2.03 | 2.33 | 2.22 | 2.13 | 2.51 |
| Turkmenistan | No data | No data | No data | No data | No data | No data | No data | No data |
| Ukraine | 66 | 2.85 | 2.41 | 2.69 | 2.72 | 2.85 | 3.15 | 3.31 |
| Uzbekistan | 117 | 2.46 | 2.25 | 2.25 | 2.38 | 2.39 | 2.53 | 2.96 |

*Source:* World Bank 2012.

**Figure 2.2  Logistics Performance Score, by Gross National Income Per Capita, Central Asia and Other Countries, 2011**

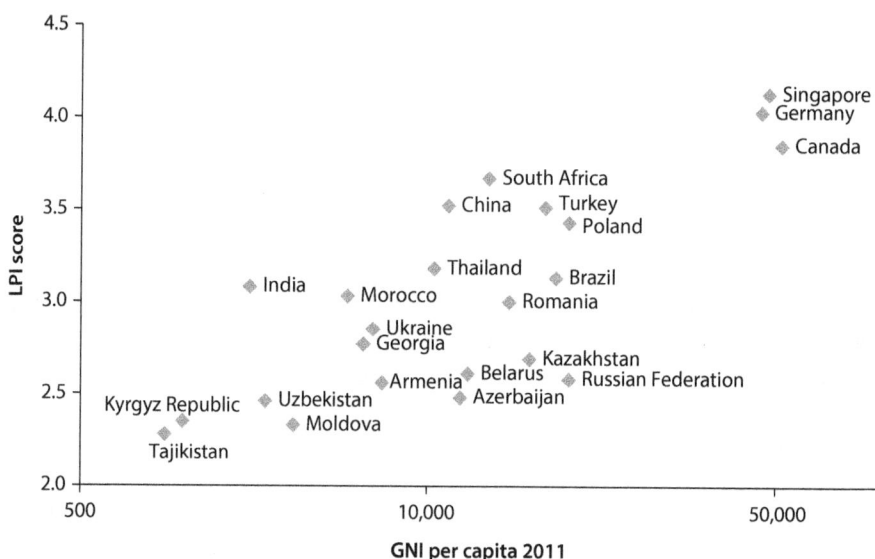

*Source:* Based on World Bank LPI and World Development Indicators.
*Note:* GNI = gross national income.

and (2) Belarus, Kazakhstan, and Russia appear to perform better than the other countries in the Central Asia region.

The comparisons across countries and dimensions (figure 2.3) show that institutional issues are at least as binding as infrastructure-related issues. Border management tends to be highly problematic, especially in Azerbaijan and Russia. Institutional reforms in areas such as customs remain a high priority despite recent progress on the ground.

In line with trade costs, the affordability of shipments tends to be lower in the smaller countries. Timeliness, as would be expected, is better in the countries closer to their main markets, which penalizes countries in Central Asia, but the tracking indicators (relevant for supply-chain reliability) are comparatively better in larger markets, where economies of scale allow for more productive and better infrastructure, especially in the railway sector.

The trends in logistics performance appear to be positive overall and reflect the increased awareness of policy makers toward logistics constraints as well as progress on the ground (figure 2.4). Infrastructure improvement and better reliability seem to drive more overall improvements seen in logistics performance than improvements in customs or quality of services.

**Figure 2.3  Intraregional Comparisons across Logistics Performance Index Dimensions, 2012**

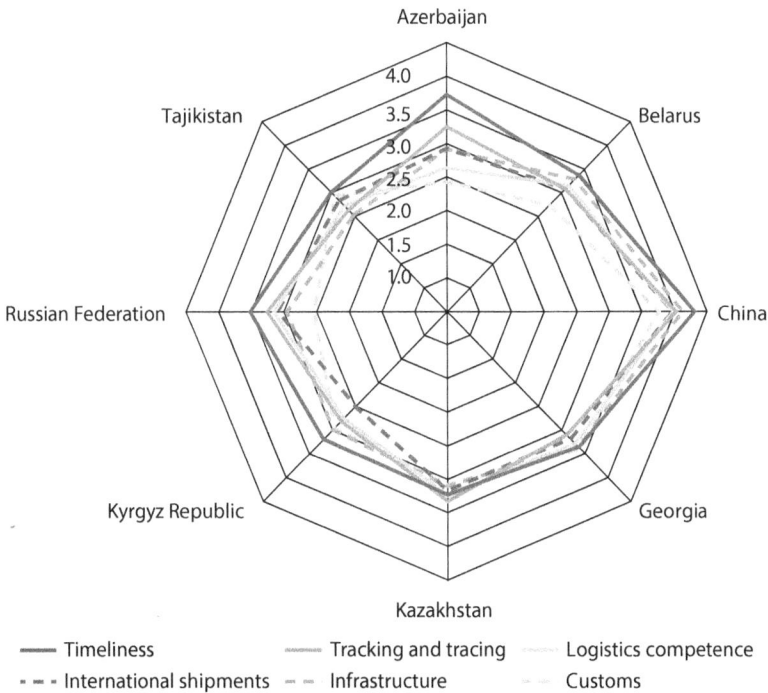

Source: World Bank 2012.
Note: Scale is from 1 to 5, and the higher the score, the better the performance.

**Figure 2.4  Country Scores as a Percentage of Highest Performer in the Overall Logistics Performance Index, 2012**

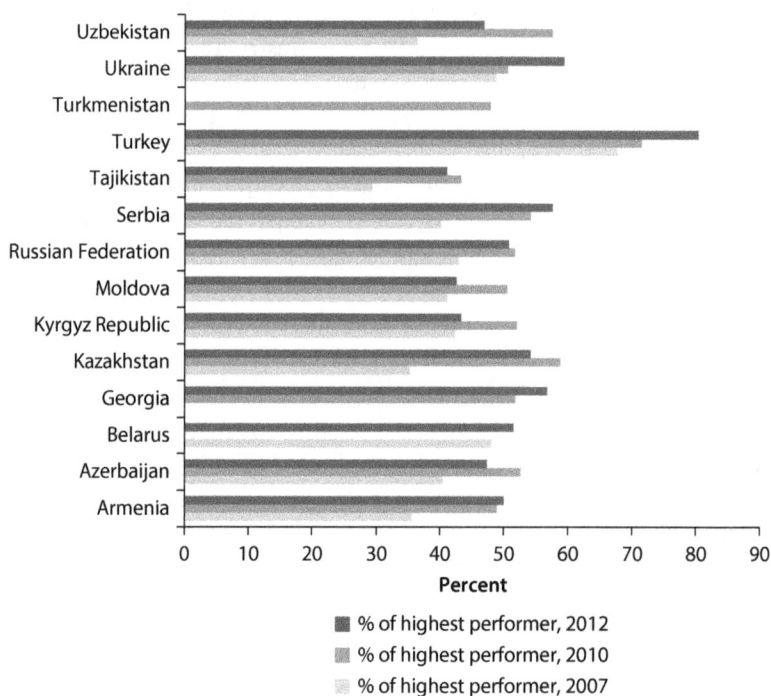

Sources: World Bank 2007, 2012.

## Two Game Changers: The Customs Union and the Rise of Trade with China

Two recent developments are likely to stimulate significant changes, both in the institutions that facilitate trade and in the private sector in the way it operates and establishes trade and transport connections in the region.

The first is the creation of the Eurasian Customs Union, which, from the perspective of the private sector, seems to have had some positive impacts on at least the northern routes in the FSU since 2012. The Customs Union (CU) has a direct facilitation impact, since customs control between borders of the Union members has been phased out. When trading with non-Union partners, the transit system in the Union is also simplified, acting like one large national transit system common to the countries in the Union. The CU also facilitates the integration of transport services (for example, railways) and improves the possibility for trucks to operate across borders (see box 2.3).

The second major development is the strong interest of the government of China to develop and facilitate overland trade with the region as part of

## Box 2.3  Legislation of the Customs Union

Ten major sources of customs legislation are used in the Eurasian Economic Community (EurAsEC) Customs Union:

1. The Treaty Establishing the Eurasian Economic Community of October 10, 2000.
2. The Agreement Establishing an Integrated Customs Territory and Formation of a Customs Union of October 6, 2007.
3. The Agreement on the Customs Union Commission of October 6, 2007.
4. The Common Customs Tariff of the Customs Union of the Republic of Belarus, Republic of Kazakhstan, and Russia.
5. The common nontariff regulations (unified list of goods whose import/export is subject to prohibitions/limitations imposed by Customs Union [CU] member states within the framework of the EurAsEC in relation to trade with third countries and having regard to the rule on limitations).
6. The Customs Code of the Customs Union 2010 (the CU CC).
7. Resolutions of the Customs Union Commission regulating legal relationships within the CU in accordance with the CU CC and international treaties of the member states and having direct effect.
8. International treaties.
9. The customs codes, resolutions, laws, and regulations of CU member states.
10. General legal principles.

Various agreements between the governments of Belarus, Kazakhstan, and Russia on customs clearance have been signed, including the agreement of December, 12, 2008, on the types of customs procedures and customs regimes; the agreement of December 12, 2008, on the procedure for goods customs declaration, and Resolution No. 4 from December, 12, 2008, on the formation of a legal environment for the CU within the framework of the EurAsEC. This resolution includes an attachment containing the following agreements and protocols:

- Protocol on the conditions and procedure of application, in exceptional circumstances, of import customs duties that differ from the rates of the common customs tariff.
- Agreement on the conditions and mechanism of tariff quota implementation.
- Protocol on the provision of tariff exemptions.
- Protocol on the common system of tariff preferences within the CU.
- Agreement on the procedure for declaring goods.
- Agreement on the procedure for the calculation and payment of customs charges in the CU member states.
- Agreement on the procedure for customs clearance and control in CU member states.
- Agreement on the types of customs procedures and regimes.
- Protocol on the uniform application of valuation rules for CU imports and exports.
- Agreement on the procedure for declaring the value of CU imports and exports.

*box continues next page*

**Box 2.3  Legislation of the Customs Union** *(continued)*

- Agreement on the procedure for verifying the correct valuation of CU imports and exports.
- Protocol on the exchange of information required for determining and verifying the customs valuation between customs agencies of Belarus, Kazakhstan, and Russia.
- Agreement on the rules for establishing the source of goods originating from developing and the least developed countries.

*Source:* Krotov 2010.

**Figure 2.5  Decreasing Nonenergy Trade Costs with China, Nonenergy Trade, 2000–10**

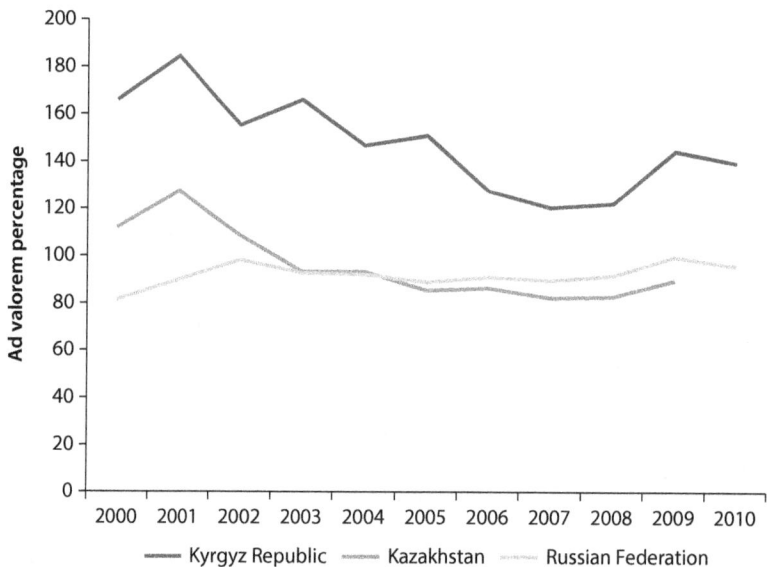

*Source:* Based on World Bank UNESCAP trade costs data set.

its strategy to further develop its western provinces. Major rail infrastructure is being completed to increase the capacity toward Kazakhstan and the Kyrgyz Republic. Special zones are being created at borders such as Khorgos/Altynkol (the province of Xinjiang in China and Almaty Oblast in Kazakhstan). This policy already shows itself in the gradual reorientation toward China of the trade of the eastern Central Asian countries, such as Kazakhstan and the Kyrgyz Republic. The share of China as a trading partner (excluding energy) has doubled since 2000 in Kazakhstan, essentially at the expense of Europe, and the trade costs with China for both Kazakhstan and the Kyrgyz Republic have fallen more than for Russia (see figures 2.5 and 2.6).

**Figure 2.6  Trade Costs of Kazakhstan with Its Main Trading Partners, 2000–09**

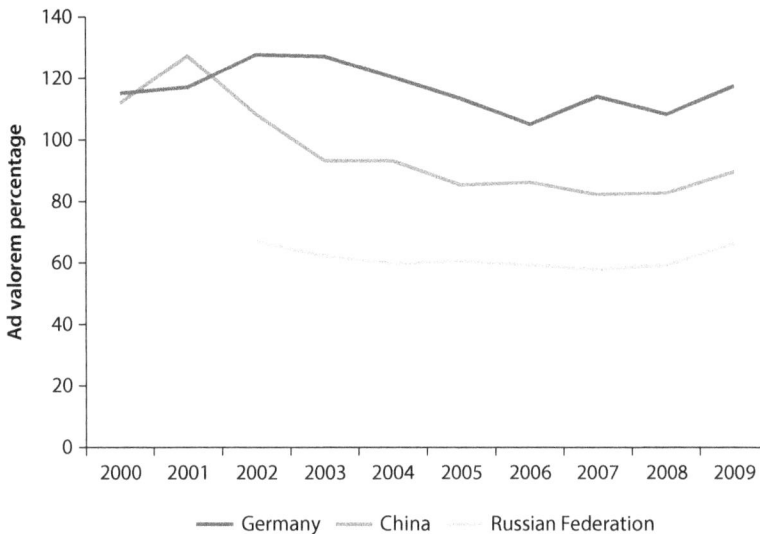

*Source:* Based on World Bank UNESCAP trade costs data set.

## Notes

1. The second and third sections also appear in World Bank (2014) *Diversified Development: Making the Most of Natural Resources in Eurasia*, which describes the broader perspective on the constraints to diversification of the regional economies.

2. Lack of trade and production data for Tajikistan, Turkmenistan, and Uzbekistan explains those countries' not being in the UNESCAP–World Bank trade costs database.

## References

Arvis, Jean-François, Yann Duval, Ben Shepherd, and Chorthip Utoktham. 2013. "Trade Costs in the Developing World." World Bank, Washington, DC.

Krotov, Igor. 2010. "Customs Union between the Republic of Belarus, the Republic of Kazakhstan and the Russian Federation within the Framework of the Eurasian Economic Community." *World Customs Journal* 5 (2).

World Bank. 2007. *Connecting to Compete: Trade Logistics in the Global Economy*. World Bank, Washington, DC.

———. 2012. *Connecting to Compete: Trade Logistics in the Global Economy 2012*. World Bank, Washington, DC.

———. 2013. "Republic of Uzbekistan—Trade Logistics and Supply Chain Performance." Case Studies from the Automotive Sector, Fertilizer Industry, and Cotton-Based Products. World Bank, Washington, DC.

———. 2014. *Diversified Development. Making the Most of Natural Resources in Eurasia*. Washington, DC: World Bank.

# CHAPTER 3

# Rail Freight Transit along the Modern Silk Route

Central Asian countries depend on transport connections on an intercontinental scale, which would typically use maritime services. The land route from Chongqing in the western province of Sichuan to Germany at a distance of 10,500 kilometers (km) is comparable in length to the trans-Pacific route from China to the U.S. west coast. Almaty, the main economic center on the modern Silk Route, is by land as distant to Western Europe as Western Europe is to the U.S. east coast (6,000 km). The distance between Almaty and major economic centers in China compares with crossing the United States from coast to coast (4,500 km). This is why land transport corridors through Central Asia are rarely used for transport connections between East Asia and Europe: almost all goods (99 percent in volume) are shipped by sea (Emerson and Vinokurov 2009).

Examples can be cited of quite efficient overland transportation by rail or truck over comparable distances. However, they are mostly within a particular country such as Canada, China, or the Russian Federation. In contrast, the modern Silk Route is about transit routes crossing many borders, whether speaking about supply connectivity through Central Asia or to Central Asia. The existence of borders is a source of fragmentation of the supply chain, which raises costs. The potential, development, and operation of transit routes along the Silk Route described in this chapter is dependent upon the existence of transit systems (or a framework for them).

Rail transit routes to and through Central Asia go primarily via Kazakhstan as the pivot transit country and can serve two complementary purposes. The first is to support the trade of Kazakhstan and the other Central Asian countries with Russia and Europe or with China through the Dostyk or Khorgos border crossing. The second is to support the Euro-Asian transit trade through the same routes. The transcontinental transit flow is comparatively a smaller part of the flow to Central Asia, and this route is in competition with the northern route through the Far East and Siberia.

## Rail Transport as the Backbone of Central Asian Connectivity

Rail transport provides the backbone for international freight transport in bulk and in containers, connecting Central Asian economies to markets. During the time of the Soviet Union, rail transport was considered the major unifying factor in economic activity, accounting for 70 percent and at times even 85 percent of its total freight transport (Strong and Meyer 1996). To date, its share in the transportation market ranges from over 60 percent in Kazakhstan (including domestic transport) up to 80–90 percent in Tajikistan and Uzbekistan (see table 3.1).

The republics of Kazakhstan and Uzbekistan, the largest economies in the region and the countries with the most developed rail networks, carry the greatest volumes of freight transported by rail in Central Asia. However, the share of transit transportation is rather small, in particular in Kazakhstan, where it accounts for only 6 percent of all freight traffic, domestic and international combined. However, Kazakhstan continues to occupy, and wants to reinforce, a central position as a transit country between the Kyrgyz Republic, Tajikistan, and Uzbekistan and their major trading partners of China, Europe, and Russia. Russia is the major country of origin, accounting for 48 percent of all transport in transit, whereas Uzbekistan is the second largest country of origin and the largest recipient country (33 percent) (Kulipanova 2012).

Although the traffic flows mainly move along north-south routes, the route along the east-west direction is gaining importance in terms of volumes transported. Freight transported to the region from China and vice versa passed through Kazakhstan and in particular Dostyk/Alashankou until the second half of 2012, when the new crossing point at Khorgos was opened. The two principal cargoes are, first, minerals imported from Kazakhstan to Urumqi and other relatively close destinations in western China's Xinjiang Province, and second, containers from the eastern ports of China (either from overseas or from Chinese consignees), principally Lianyungang, Qingdao, and Tianjin, as well as some from Urumqi (see figure 3.1). One of the most active container transit traffic routes

**Table 3.1  Rail Freight Volume and Turnover in Central Asia**

| Million tons | Kazakhstan (2012) | Kyrgyz Republic (2012) | Tajikistan (2008) | Turkmenistan (2012) | Uzbekistan (2008) |
|---|---|---|---|---|---|
| Domestic | 158.7 | – | 0 | – | 54.2 |
| Export | 100.9 | 0.62 | 0.9 | 13.33 | 5.1 |
| Import | 18.78 | 5.72 | 4.5 | 2.71 | 8.0 |
| Transit | 16.3 | 0 | 9.0* | 4.02 | 11.0 |
| Total | 294.7 | 6.34 | 14.4 | 20.06 | 78.3 |
| Million ton-km | Kazakhstan (2012) | Kyrgyz Republic (2006) | Tajikistan (2008) | Turkmenistan (2008) | Uzbekistan (2010) |
| Total | 235,900 | 1.9 | 128.15 | 9.20 | 23,404 |

*Sources:* Based on various sources, including Kulipanova 2012; TRACECA Study; Turkmenistan State Customs Service.

The Eurasian Connection  •  http://dx.doi.org/10.1596/978-0-8213-9912-5

from China's ports through Dostyk (Alashankou) is traffic from the Republic of Korea to Uzbekistan, and within that, the automobile parts moving to the General Motors plant at Assaka, 17 km southwest of Andijan in the Ferghana Valley (see table 3.2).

The nontransit freight in 2010 to and from Central Asia and China was 13.6 million tonnes, of which 11.2 million were transported by rail. Of this,

**Figure 3.1  Railway Border Crossing Traffic at Alashankou (Kazakhstan–China Border), 2002–10**

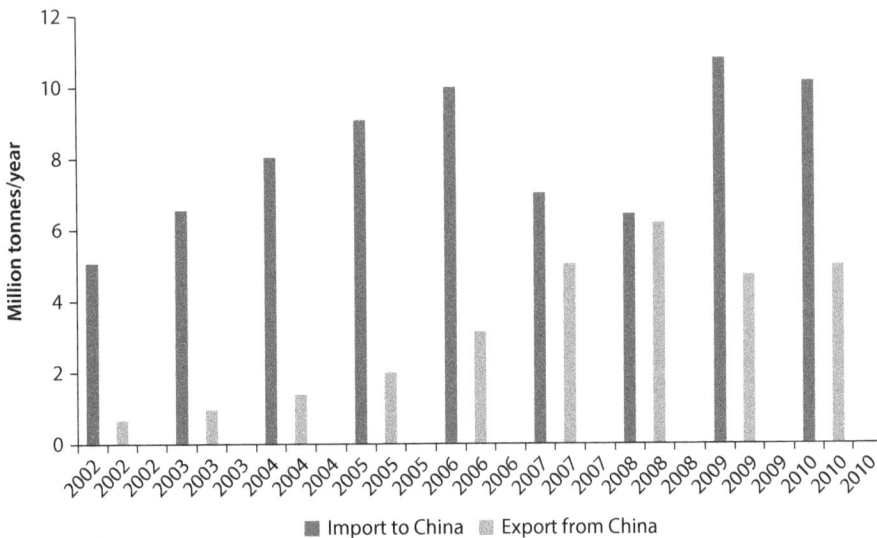

Source: Yearbook of China Transportation and Communications 2005–11.

**Table 3.2  Exports from the Republic of Korea to Central Asia, 2011–12**

Thousand tons

| | Afghanistan | | Kyrgyz Republic | | Kazakhstan | | Tajikistan | | Turkmenistan | | Uzbekistan | | Total | |
|---|---|---|---|---|---|---|---|---|---|---|---|---|---|---|
| | 2011 | 2012 | 2011 | 2012 | 2011 | 2012 | 2011 | 2012 | 2011 | 2012 | 2011 | 2012 | 2011 | 2012 |
| Tobacco products | 14 | 13 | 1 | 0 | 2 | 3 | 0 | 0 | 0 | 0 | 0 | 0 | 16 | 17 |
| Plastic products | 0 | 0 | 14 | 12 | 18 | 18 | 5 | 1 | 3 | 2 | 47 | 48 | 87 | 81 |
| Rubber manufacturing | 0 | 0 | 0 | 1 | 4 | 4 | 0 | 0 | 0 | 0 | 7 | 9 | 11 | 14 |
| Artificial fibers | 1 | 2 | 0 | 0 | 11 | 21 | 0 | 0 | 0 | 0 | 0 | 0 | 13 | 23 |
| Knitted fabrics | 0 | 2 | 7 | 7 | 26 | 32 | 0 | 0 | 0 | 0 | 5 | 5 | 39 | 46 |
| Iron and steel | 0 | 0 | 1 | 0 | 0 | 1 | 0 | 0 | 4 | 4 | 33 | 35 | 38 | 40 |
| Steel manufacturing | 0 | 0 | 0 | 0 | 0 | 0 | 0 | 0 | 13 | 6 | 3 | 6 | 16 | 13 |
| Machinery | 0 | 0 | 1 | 3 | 67 | 57 | 2 | 3 | 16 | 9 | 41 | 40 | 127 | 111 |
| Vehicles/parts | 1 | 1 | 14 | 18 | 9 | 10 | 8 | 9 | 3 | 8 | 126 | 134 | 161 | 181 |
| Furniture | 0 | 0 | 0 | 0 | 0 | 1 | 0 | 0 | 0 | 0 | 8 | 9 | 8 | 10 |
| Other | 3 | 7 | 5 | 5 | 33 | 24 | 1 | 1 | 17 | 9 | 39 | 38 | 99 | 84 |
| Total | 20 | 26 | 44 | 46 | 170 | 171 | 16 | 13 | 44 | 34 | 298 | 308 | 592 | 598 |

Source: Customs Data, China, Kazakhstan, and the Republic of Korea.

The Eurasian Connection • http://dx.doi.org/10.1596/978-0-8213-9912-5

8.7 million tonnes represent imports from Kazakhstan to China. The remaining 2.6 million tonnes included 0.6 million tonnes to and from Russia, 0.5 million tonnes to and from Uzbekistan, and 1.1 million tonnes to and from the Kyrgyz Republic. Traffic to and from the other Central Asian countries and Europe totaled 0.5 million tonnes, largely to and from Tajikistan.

The countries of destination (and to a lesser extent origin) of traffic through Dostyk-Alashankou are the Kyrgyz Republic, Tajikistan, and Uzbekistan. The absolute volumes, however, are not large. By far the biggest component of transit traffic from China's ports through Alashankou is traffic from the Republic of Korea to Uzbekistan, and within that, the automobile parts moving to the GM plant at Assaka. The Kyrgyz Republic relies less on rail transit through Uzbekistan because more than half of its imports and exports are carried through the northern branch linked to Kazakhstan. Almost all the 600,000 tonnes of transit freight is reportedly moved by rail. Most of the traffic from Korea is containerizable, with the possible exception of the iron and steel, and thus, with Afghan, Tajik, and Turkmen traffic, it represents around 30,000–35,000 twenty-foot equivalent units (TEU) each way. Much of this traffic is carried in a dedicated block train from Lianyungang to Alashankou-Dostyk.[1]

This analysis demonstrates the relative importance of Kazakhstan as a transit country for imports from Asia to other Central Asian countries, in particular the Kyrgyz Republic and Uzbekistan. The volumes of transit are comparable in Kazakhstan and Uzbekistan, but the share of transit is larger in Uzbekistan. Uzbekistan is the major country for intraregional rail transit in Central Asia. Neighboring Central Asia and Russia account for nearly 74 percent of all transit carried through Uzbekistan.[2] Tajikistan particularly is entirely dependent on Uzbekistan's railway network because its three isolated domestic railway lines, which make up the country's entire railway system, connect to Uzbekistan's railway network. The Kyrgyz Republic relies less on rail transit through Uzbekistan because more than half of its imports and exports are carried through the northern branch linked to Kazakhstan.

Transit volumes are low on other international rail corridors. Various sources (TRACECA 2010) indicate that the railway line from Turkmenistan to the Islamic Republic of Iran (Serakh) and farther on to the Persian Gulf is mostly used for transit to and from China, the Islamic Republic of Iran, and Russia and by Uzbekistan to transport its cotton to the Iranian port of Bandar Abbas. In the first half of 2010, the overall freight volume through this corridor amounted to 3.2 million tons, of which only 28 percent were goods in transit. However, it appears that this percentage most likely refers to freight carried through the intermodal Transcaspian and Caucasian routes rather than overland through Central Asia (Kulipanova 2012). The Transcaspian sea routes, including Transport Corridor Europe-Caucasus-Asia (TRACECA), involve the ports of Aktau in Kazakhstan and Turkmenbashi in Turkmenistan, which are important for export-oriented trade. To date, the railway transport routes through Central Asia appear to be mainly used to serve regional transit destined to or originated from Russia/Europe and China/East Asia.

## Transit Trade (Transcontinental): Institutional Arrangements

What does it take to establish the long-distance transit connections that are vital to the landlocked countries of Central Asia? This topic is traditionally looked at from the perspective of the trade access problem of landlocked countries, which coincidentally is the focus of the Almaty Programme of Action, an international initiative started in 2003 (see box 3.1). The two most obvious requirements of a transit system are the existence of a physical road or rail infrastructure, and the openness of borders to the movement of merchandise and vehicles, which does not always fully exist in the region.

Institutional arrangements, which define how goods move in transit and what rules apply to vehicles (trucks or trains) transporting them in transit across several territories, constitute the transit system that makes long-distance transportation feasible. A transit system combines the implementation in countries of transit of well-known and codified principles as well as a component of regional cooperation, such as targeting a specific border crossing.

Transport by rail in either sealed containers or freight wagons has a comparative advantage over trucking, because it offers a higher degree of customs security (one operator, constrained routes and facilities) and usually requires less paperwork (for example, waiver of guarantees for national rail companies).

---

### Box 3.1 The Almaty Programme of Action, 2003

The Almaty Conference (2003) highlighted five priority areas for landlocked countries:

*Transit policy and regulatory frameworks:* Both landlocked and transit countries should review regulatory frameworks and establish regional transport corridors.

*Infrastructure development:* Landlocked countries need to develop multimodal networks (rail, road, air, and pipeline infrastructure projects).

*Trade and transport facilitation:* Landlocked countries need to implement the international conventions and instruments designed to facilitate transit trade (including the World Trade Organization).

*Development assistance:* The international community needs to assist by (1) providing technical support, (2) encouraging foreign direct investment, and (3) increasing official development assistance.

*Implementation and review:* Procedures for monitoring the implementation of transit instruments and conducting a comprehensive review of their implementation must be established in due course.

The 2008 midterm review confirmed these priorities but recognized a substantial change in the environment, stressing the need "to look at new approaches … directly linked to transit" and to consider "developments in the transport sector." Among these are port developments, intermodal transport operators, and increased use of information and communication technologies (ICTs) to program and manage operations and check traffic at border control points.

*Sources:* Almaty Programme of Action 2003; and key issues for the preparatory meeting of the midterm review (UNCTAD 2003).

---

The documentation is unified within the former Soviet Union (see table 3.3 for details).

Notwithstanding the actual facilitation problems observed on the ground, the main challenge to efficient transit may not be the institutional organization of transit but rather the actual capability of rail and trucking operators in Central Asia to offer seamless services over long distances. This is a matter not only of having performing local providers but also of fostering networks of partner services to cover the full distance. For instance, the cross-border integration of railway operations between national companies and the improvement of their operational performance are critical to transit supply chains.

This integration can be done either by the railways themselves or by international freight forwarders. International freight forwarders have the comparative advantage of serving clients from origin and destinations such as multinational companies active in both Europe and China. They typically contract freight services and transport capacities with national railways and local trucking companies. Their role is to integrate services over long distances, being able to track and trace cargo in transit across several territories and borders. Therefore they can address numerous coordination and information challenges better than the transport operators taken separately (box 3.2).

## Euro-Asian (Transcontinental) Transit Trade along the Modern Silk Route

Much has already been written about the potential for overland rail routes, in particular Trans-Siberian Railways (TRS; Moscow-Yekaterinburg-Omsk-Irkutsk-Zabaykalsk) (Linn 2012), but 20 years after the route became technically

**Table 3.3 Agreements on Rail Freight Transportation**

| Agreement | Description |
|---|---|
| SMGS Agreement on international rail freight transportation signed between the members of OSJD (Organization for Cooperation between Railways) http://www.railways.kz/ru/node/88 | SMGS Agreement with annexes. Among other things it contains templates for SMGS consignment note and recommendations on how to fill out the SMGS note. |
| CIS Railway Council Rules of the private freight wagon usage Klaipeda, June 19, 2001 http://www.railways.kz/ru/node/88 | Rules of usage of privately owned rail cars (not owned by the railway administrations) Registration, numbering system for railway cars Control and reporting Document templates for private car owners |
| CIS Freedom of Transit Agreement http://cis.minsk.by/reestr/ru/index.html#reestr/view /text?doc=933 | Regulates transit of goods and freight vehicles that carry transit cargo between CIS countries |

*Source:* Authors.
*Note:* CIS = Commonwealth of Independent States. OSJD is an international organization established at the Railway Ministers Conference in Sofia, Bulgaria, by the ministers responsible for railway transport on June 28, 1956. Twenty-seven countries take part in the activities of OSJD as an intergovernmental organization: Albania, Azerbaijan, Belarus, Bulgaria, China, Cuba, the Czech Republic, the Democratic People's Republic of Korea, Estonia, Georgia, Hungary, the Islamic Republic of Iran, Kazakhstan, the Kyrgyz Republic, Latvia, Lithuania, Moldova, Mongolia, Poland, Romania, Russian Federation, the Slovak Republic, Tajikistan, Turkmenistan, Ukraine, Uzbekistan, and Vietnam.

**Box 3.2  Simplification of Freight Documentation**

Deutsche Bahn (DB) Schenker has successfully tested a common consignment note on a rail shipment between China and Germany. More process improvements and more time savings are enhancing rail's competitiveness.

DB Schenker has successfully tested the use of a common consignment note for rail freight shipments between China and Europe. The first container train dispatched from China by DB Schenker under a common consignment note successfully arrived in Germany. Once the procedure is introduced on regular services, it will be possible to ensure the customer of a shorter journey time. Trains currently arriving in Duisburg from Chongqing in China's hinterland require 18 days for the journey, which is half the time required when shipping freight by sea. DB Schenker provided the service for a consumer electronics manufacturer that has been sending container trains for two years from Chongqing along the approximately 11,000 km route through China, Kazakhstan, Russia, Belarus, and Poland to Germany. DB Schenker and the rail operator YuXinOu (Chongqing) Logistics Co., a joint venture, had joint overall responsibility for the preparation and completion of this test. Together with Trans Eurasia Logistics GmbH, a joint venture between Deutsche Bahn and RZD, DB Schenker has been pushing for the introduction of a single consignment note for the entire journey and will now be one of the first companies able to use this procedure on this route.

"The shorter transit time that is now possible will give new impetus to the Eurasian Land Bridge and allows us to recommend ourselves to our customers as an innovative, strong and reliable partner," says Dr. Karl-Friedrich Rausch, member of the Management Board of DB Mobility Logistics AG responsible for the Transportation and Logistics Division.

On the test run from China to Europe, it has been possible to demonstrate how a common consignment note is designed to work, because the complete information required for the transit and receiver countries en route must also be included on the new common consignment note when it is issued in China. As a result, the examinations and supplementary data, which are currently required for the European sections of the route, in addition to the transcription of the consignment notes, will be eliminated in the future. This means that time spent at border crossings can be significantly reduced, with a corresponding reduction in provision and transit times. This will benefit the entire sector and enhance rail's competitiveness. The simplification of freight documents, similar to the situation in air and ocean freight, is one of the most important measures now being introduced to further reduce the journey time significantly between China and Europe. Until now, two separate consignment notes have been required for rail shipments of this kind. The simplification also opens up the possibility of using an electronic consignment note in the future.

*Source:* DB Group, November 27, 2012.

available to shippers, volumes are still low in absolute terms. The total containerized seaborne market between China and Europe in 2012 was about 5.3 million TEU westbound[3] and 3.0 million TEU eastbound. Of total westbound freight, 4.0 million TEU was from eastern China and 1.9 million TEU from southern China. Within Europe, about 30 percent of the volume is to Mediterranean ports and 70 percent to northwestern Europe. Leaving aside air and road, this represents over 98 percent of the total containerized traffic, with the largest landborne flow being on TRS to and from the Republic of Korea and Japan, which carried just 46,500 TEU in 2011 (an increase of 41 percent over 2010).[4]

Currently Euro-Asian trade along routes through Central Asia (Trans-Kazakhstan Railways [TKR] along Moscow-Yekaterinburg-Petropavlosk-Aktogay-Dostyk, also referred to as the northern Trans-Asian corridor) plays a marginal role in transcontinental container transit traffic. Since 2010 various Europe-China rail services along TKR have either begun or been given trials.

The major challenge for the future development of TKR is its competitive position in comparison to TRS, although this is less important at the moment because of small amounts of traffic in absolute terms. The development of international rail routes through the northern and eastern part of Kazakhstan depends significantly on the infrastructure condition of the relevant sections of the Russian railways (RZD).

At present, overland rail routes connecting Europe and Asia through TSR and TKR play a marginal role for transcontinental transit traffic. Although some differences of opinion exist on the future growth of Euro-Asian freight volumes to be captured by TSR and TKR, most research points to the fact that maritime transport will likely remain the dominant mode in the Europe-Asia transport market (no less than 95 percent), at least for some years to come. The low use of the land bridge for transcontinental trade has many causes.

In general, the availability, quality, costs, reliability, and frequency of container services along the transcontinental rail routes compare unfavorably with those of maritime shipping. As one would expect, in comparison to sea transport, Euro-Asian rail transport offers lower transit time at a higher price. The price level (index) from Shanghai/Beijing to Moscow is sea freight to rail as 3–5. The lead times (days) terminal to terminal from Shanghai/Beijing to Moscow are sea freight/rail freight as 33–40 days to 10–12 days.[5] Therefore, TSR and TKR are able to serve a niche market for high-value and time-sensitive cargo originating or destined from/for Chinese inland places.

The market price for transporting goods equivalent to the volume of 1 TEU by air was approximately €22,000 in 2011. For the same year, 1 TEU per sea/air is approximately half the price, around €11,000. A TEU shipped by sea costs on average €1,850 in 2008. According to one analysis, the minimum price to be charged for a container from China to Europe via railway is €2,500–€3,500 (assuming a profit of approximately 10 percent) (Bauer 2008).

Lead time from Moscow to the border crossing with China differs slightly between TKR and TSR. It is estimated that the distance from Moscow to Dostyk via TKR can be covered by a block train in eight days, using TSR (until Erenhot) in 10 days, and TSR (until Zabaykalsk) in seven days. Frequency of service for container block trains differs greatly, depending on the different operators, from daily service to twice a month.

Shorter lead time (due to shorter distance) is the valuable competitive advantage that overland rail routes such as TSR and TKR could offer for certain commodities, production locations, and customers. In addition, the time factor is an important element for rapidly growing regions that have no viable alternative to rail and road transit, as is the case for landlocked regions. Provinces of western China, such as the Xinjiang Uighur Autonomous Region, present such a case.

## Long-Distance Silk Route to Complement Shipping: Servicing Niche Markets

The Eurasian rail bridge between China and Europe offers an interesting compromise between lead time in transportation and price, between shipping and air cargo, that is currently not sufficiently catered to (figure 3.2). It offers an attractive logistics solution that allows for more flexibility than shipping and fewer costs than air freight for time-sensitive shipments between those markets for a few time-sensitive supply chains involving manufacturing production sharing, such as electronics and auto parts.

A few multinational companies have looked at the full supply chain for those specific products and worked with major forwarders to develop scheduled services (block trains). These specialized container services along TSR and TKR remain targeted company initiatives and represent a negligible 3–4 percent share (or 364,002 TEU in 2010) of total container traffic between Europe and Asia (Chamber of Commerce of the United States 2006).

What makes this road potentially attractive? So far it appears as a niche market that is a complement to the shipping routes rather than a competing solution. Interviews with companies using the rail routes (Siberia or Kazakhstan) suggest that rail transportation is used for a minority share of their freight so as to be able to smooth and reduce their inventory requirements in Asia or Europe; those

**Figure 3.2 Market Segmentation of Transportation Services on the Eurasian Link: Lead Time versus Price**

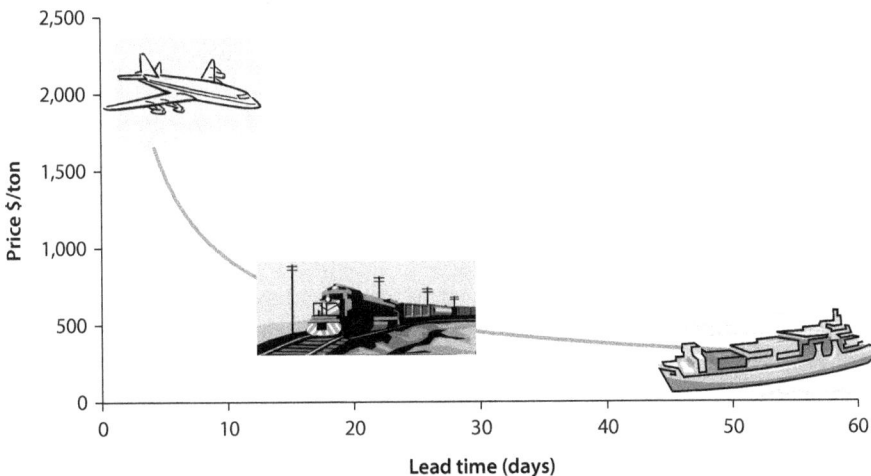

are typically associated with long lead times. German manufacturers have halved their inventory of imported engine and gear box components in their Chinese car factories, for example, by using trains for 10–20 percent of their imported inputs. However, and of particular interest to Kazakhstan and other Central Asian countries, the new Silk Road railway link route may be competitive as a primary alternative for producers from western China (for example, Sichuan or Xinjiang provinces).

Another requirement of an operational nature is that the operators provide reliable, frequent, and scheduled service that makes it compatible with the supply-chain constraints of those multinational companies using the service. Generally, the operators or group of operators can guarantee a lead time to the shippers within which the shipment can be delivered. According to interviews, DB Schenker in strategic alliance with RZD is reportedly in a position to provide a guaranteed lead time of 23 days from Germany to Manchuria along TSR.

Those specialized container services have been introduced by companies in the electronics and automobile market. Along TKR, these include Hewlett Packard, Ace, and Asus, which ran a total of 40 container trains in 2012 from Chongqing (China) to Duisburg. In early 2013 the Chongqing-Xinjiang-Duisburg container railway service (covering 11,179 km with a transit time for a single journey of 18 days) also launched its first return service and was expected to arrive in Chongqing in mid-March, carrying 41 TEU of Ford auto parts. It is expected that in 2013 Chongqing-bound service will be increased to once a week, and the return (Germany-bound) service will be introduced three times a week. Additionally, it has been reported that the rate of the service has been lowered from $0.9 to $0.7 per TEU per km, with collaboration among the government of Chongqing, China Railway Group, and the logistics operators from countries along the line.

Since November 2011 container trains have traveled daily along TSR from Germany (Leipzig) to China (Shenyang) to transport parts and components to BMW's Shenyang plant in Liaoning Province, where they are used for the assembly of BMW vehicles (Deutsche Bahn Schenker 2011). Since January 2012, under the product name of Trans-Eurasia Express, two container trains are initially to travel weekly to link Xiangtang, which lies about 700 km north of Hong Kong SAR, China, with Hamburg, Duisburg, and Nuremberg for Fujitsu Siemens Computers, traveling 12,000 km by rail to Germany.

To date, the business model of the Eurasian rail container link consists of scheduled block trains for single shippers, operating from plant to plant. This is a major simplification of the logistics in terms of scheduling contracting, documentation, and customs. The next step for the development of those routes would be to be able to offer the same type of scheduled and reliable service for customers shipping less than full train loads. The route(s) should be able to evolve from a "customer-driven model" toward a "retail model" (see box 3.3 and figure 3.3). The latter is based on agreements between international logistics companies, such as DB Schenker and Sinotrans and the rail operators and

## Box 3.3  Existing Models for Freight Transportation

The organization of long-distance transit connection evolved naturally into three successive types:

1. The *Customer-Driven Model* is the current level of organization, based on *full trains organized by manufacturing companies* to serve their own need to transport inputs and finished products. Examples include companies such as Hewlett Packard (HP), General Motors (GM), Daewoo, and BMW. Companies form the entire train to transport their goods. They deal directly with transport operators and customs of the transit country with the participation of local agents (freight forwarders and brokers).

    For HP, shipping one container by train costs about $10,000, which is about one-third the price of air transit and is about twice the cost of shipping by sea. Since 2011 HP has transported 4 million notebook computers along the 11,179-km rail route, from its factory in Chongqing through Kazakhstan, Russia, Belarus, and Poland to Duisburg, Germany. A separate line from China's northeast links up with TSR, which runs 9,288 km from Vladivostok to Moscow. It takes only 21 days for products from a factory in Chongqing to reach Western Europe by rail. Electronics companies including Foxconn and Acer, both with factories in Chongqing, are also shipping to Europe by rail.

    In the case of GM, the company relies on the supply chains that have been developed by Daewoo in the past. Most of the suppliers are Korean, and imports from the Republic of Korea amount to about 30,000 twenty-foot equivalent units per year. Nearly all of these are shipped from Busan, unloaded in the Lianyungang port, and then transported in block trains to Angren. These trains operate twice weekly under an agreement with China Railways. Because of the unreliability on this route in 2012, GM Uzbekistan established an alternative weekly service on the Transsiberian route from Nakhodka even though this route is about 2,000 km longer. The shipments are arranged by international freight forwarders, whereas the movements within Uzbekistan are arranged by the Angren Logistics Center and DHL. The transit time from the unloading port to Tashkent is typically about 15 days.

2. The *Retail Model* is based on agreements between international logistics companies such as DB Schenker and Sinotrans and the operators and agencies in the country of transit. The logistics companies organize scheduled full trains and sell the capacity to their clients, which are manufacturing or trading companies. Under the "Global Partner" project, Kazakhstan Temir Jolu (KTZ) aims to establish cooperation with world transport and logistics companies and large producers to increase transportation of goods to/from/via Kazakhstan. KTZ has already signed numerous memoranda with companies such as Sinotrans and DB Schenker.

    DB Schenker has operated trains from Germany to China since September 2011. It supplies automotive parts and components to BMW's new automobile plant in Shenyang on behalf of the car manufacturer. One train loaded with 40 containers heads eastward for BMW from the sidings at the Leipzig logistics center every day. More than 120 DB Schenker Rail container trains loaded with over 4,700 containers have traveled

*box continues next page*

The Eurasian Connection  •  http://dx.doi.org/10.1596/978-0-8213-9912-5

**Box 3.3  Existing Models for Freight Transportation** *(continued)*

> from Leipzig to Shenyan for BMW so far. One BMW train also departs for Shenyang from Wackersdorf every week.
>
> 3. The *Wholesale Model* is based on railway companies providing fully specialized multi-modal logistics services This model is popular in North America; examples include such companies as CSX, Canadian Pacific, and Union Pacific.

*Sources:* Expert interviews, Bloomberg Businessweek, Global Economics 2012; DB Schenker, Canadian Pacific.

**Figure 3.3  Existing Models for Long-Distance Freight Transportation**

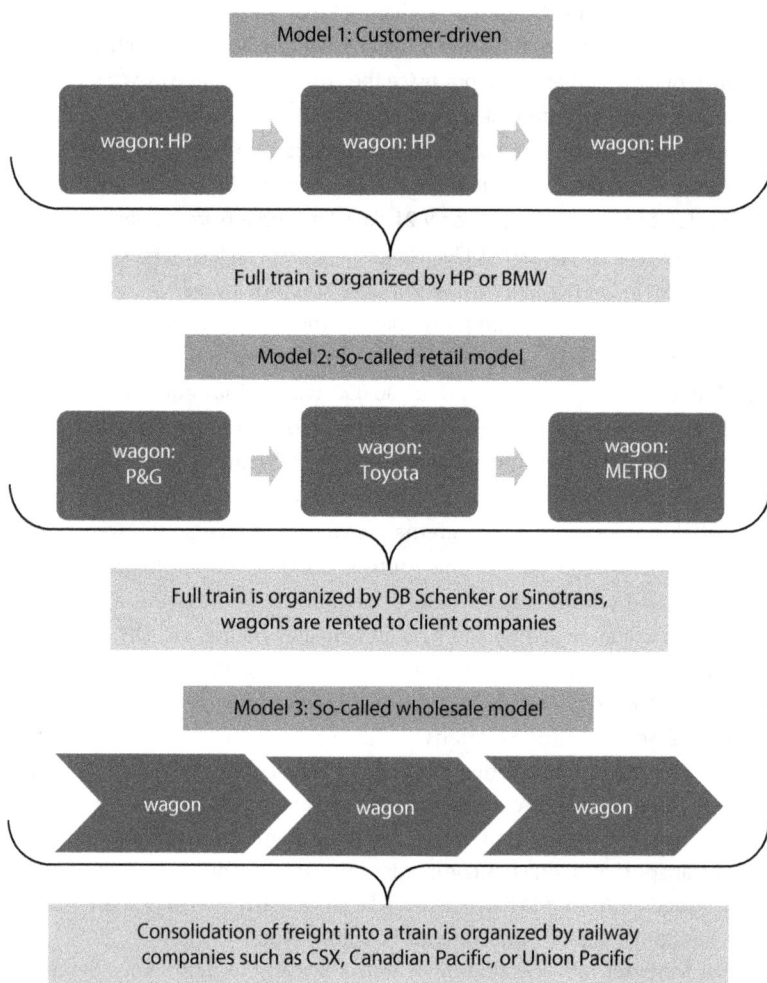

agencies in the country of transit. As of 2013, the offer of consolidated "retail" services is limited (table 3.4).

One of the important issues that impact the frequency of services is the lack of spare capacity along the routes and possible capacity bottlenecks. Reportedly enough capacity exists to increase services along TSR and TKR.

**Table 3.4 Scheduled Container Rail Services (Block Trains) Operating between Europe and Asia (as of Mid-2013)**

| Advertised service name | Route description | Operator | Frequency |
|---|---|---|---|
| **Central Asian route** | | | |
| Kazakhstan Vector | Berlin<br>Brest-Illijezk (Russian Federation)-Arys (Kazakhstan)<br>Almaty-Dostyk Alshankou<br>Urumqi | Kaztrans services in cooperation with Belarus's official transport and logistics company "Belintertrans-Transport-Logistic-Centre" | Two times per week plus regular chartered operations<br>Total 14 each week on this route<br>11,800 km<br>Lead time of 26 days |
| **Siberian route** | | | |
| Trans-Eurasia Express OstWind | Berlin<br>Moscow Novosibirsk<br>Zabailkalsk (Russia-China Border<br>Harbin, Shenyang, Beijing) | TEL Trans-Eurasia Logistics, a joint venture between Deutsche Bahn AG and the Russian Railways (RZD). Its other partners are TransContainer, Polzug, and Kombiverkehr.<br>Competitor InterRail Services (Ostwind) | One each week plus regular chartered trains (total over 20)<br>13,000 km<br>Lead time of 22 days |

*Source:* Based on various information sources, including European Commission 2012.

According to information from the Coordinating Council on Transsiberian Transportation (CCTT), TRS is capable of transporting up to 130 million tons per year, including about 500,000–600,000 containers of import/export cargo and 250,000–300,000 containers for transit. TSR capacity is presently 360,000 TEU, and an extension to 1 million TEU per year may be possible. The comparatively high capacity of trains on TSR is seen as an advantage. Every train on TSR consists of 57 wagons, each transporting two 40-foot containers. This is equivalent to 228 TEU per train.[6]

For TKR, there seems to be enough spare capacity on the railways to introduce new train services, because the majority of the oil, which was formerly transported by rail in Kazakhstan, has been redistributed to pipelines. Container trains in Kazakhstan (as generally in Central Asia) are frequently intermingled with mixed or bulk freight trains. Therefore, the lead time of container trains also depends on the frequency of service and the volume and speed of the general railway traffic, impacting container train runs. Additionally, the economic specialization of the main centers situated along TKR is oriented toward heavy industrial activities, such as energy products, steel, (petro) chemicals, and agricultural products; thus, it is expected that bulk trains will have the lead in the development of this route. Nonetheless, a potential exists for container train development, which is supported by the government of Kazakhstan, because the number of container block trains that run through the territory of Kazakhstan is increasing steadily.

With varying degrees of enthusiasm, different researchers agree on certain characteristics that serve to provide rail with an opportunity to provide a reliable complement to seaborne logistics, and to a certain extent develop an advantage over road for shorter distances. These include (1) origins and destinations to and from western and central China (for example, as far east as Chongqing), (2) origins and destinations in Eastern Europe (as far west as Berlin), and (3) guaranteed lead time consolidated services. In addition, traffic along the Europe-Asia rail routes will reinforce the necessity to improve land transport rail routes as a source of development for the countries concerned. This is also expected to substantially benefit connecting centers of growth within the region.

## Notes

1. While many of these figures from the various sources vary by quite large margins, they are in the main sufficiently consistent. It is well known that customs data are difficult to reconcile, but the orders of magnitude are consistent between sources for most trade flows except for Kyrgyz Republic imports from China, for which "shadow imports" are a known problem.

2. The southern route to Afghanistan also gained importance as the Central Asian countries joined the Northern Distribution Network to support North Atlantic Treaty Organization (NATO) operations in Afghanistan. It accounted for nearly 14 percent of all transit in Uzbekistan in 2008 (Kulipanova 2012).

3. All figures are for loaded containers only. The TEU statistics have been converted into tons assuming that 1 TEU averages 10 tons.

4. Most of the traffic transported along TSR consists of imports to and exports from the Russian Federation (more than 90 percent), and the share of transit remains minimal. The total volume of international traffic along the TRS in general amounted to nearly 70 million tonnes during the first eight months of 2011 and has increased by 0.8 percent compared with the same period in 2010.

5. TEE Trans Eurasia Express: Ein Neues Produkt zwischen Asien and Europa/Transportloesungen (Presentation), Trans Eurasia Logistics. Berlin: GmbH, 2009.

6. http://www.retrack.eu/downloadables/Deliverables/D13.2-Public-Report%20on%20potential%20for%20Eurasia%20land%20bridge%20rail%20corridors-FINAL-25042012.pdf, p. 110.

## References

Bauer, Kurt. 2008. "Is There a Market for a Container Train China-Western Europe?" *Railway Market. CEE Review* No. 1.

*Bloomberg Businessweek, Global Economics.* 2012. "The Silk Railroad of China-Europe Trade." December 20.

Chamber of Commerce of the United States. 2006. "Land Transport Options between Europe and Asia: Commercial Feasibility Study." Chamber of Commerce of the United States, Washington, DC. http://www.internationaltransportforum.org/Proceedings/Border2009/USChamberOfCommerce2.pdf.

China, Government of. 2005–11. *Yearbook of China Transportation and Communications.* Beijing: Yearbook of China Transportation and Communications Press.

Deutsche Bahn Schenker. 2011. "By Rail from Leipzig to China." *DB Schenker Newsletter* No. 65/11.

DB Group. November 29, 2012. http://www.worldcargonews.com/htm/w20121129 .922510.htm.

Emerson, Michael, and Evgeny Vinokurov. 2009. "Optimisation of Central Asian and Eurasian Trans-Continental Land Transport Corridors." EUCAM Working Paper 7, December 17.

European Commission. 2012. "Potential for Eurasia Land Bridge Corridors & Logistics Developments along the Corridors." Brussels.

Kulipanova, Elena. 2012. "International Transport in Central Asia: Understanding the Patterns of (Non)-Cooperation." Working Paper 2, University of Central Asia, Bishkek.

Linn, Johannes. 2012. "Central Asian Regional Integration and Cooperation: Reality or Mirage?" In *Eurasian Integration Yearbook 2012*, edited by Evgeny Vinokurov, 96–117. Almaty: Eurasian Development Bank.

Strong, John S., and John R. Meyer, with Clell G. Harral and Graham Smith. 1996. *Moving to Market: Restructuring Transport in the Former Soviet Union.* Cambridge, MA: Harvard University Press.

TRACECA. 2010. International Logistics Centres/Nodes Network, Central Asia at the Republic of Kazakhstan, Kyrgyz Republic, Republic of Tajikistan, Republic of Uzbekistan and the Republic of Turkmenistan, EuropeAid/125727/C/SER/Multi. http://www.traceca-org.org/en/home/.

UNCTAD. 2003. "Report of the International Ministerial Conference of Landlocked and Transit Developing Countries and Donor Countries and International Financial and Development Institutions on Transit Transport Cooperation." Almaty, Kazakhstan, August, 28 and 29.

## CHAPTER 4

# Road Transport Connections along the Modern Silk Route

This chapter focuses on internal connectivity within the Central Asian countries along the modern Silk Route with a particular focus on cross-border and international road transportation. The regional supply chains depend not only on the physical infrastructure (roads), but also on the development of freight services and the rules organizing transport and cross-border movement of goods in transit in the region.

## Connecting Central Asia at a Regional Level

The share of international transportation by trucks as compared with rail freight wagons is lower in all Central Asian countries (with the exception of the Kyrgyz Republic), where it accounts on average for less than 6 percent. In general terms, road transport is the preferred option for short-haul and sometimes even for longer distances. Currently road transport is favored for time-sensitive items (fruits and vegetables, textiles and clothing, and other consumer goods), but rail transport is preferred for bulky goods over long distances (such as building and construction materials, wood, equipment, and motors and motor parts).

The importance of road transport is nevertheless increasing, in particular for regional and cross-border connections. The geography of the most heavily used routes again underlines the importance of the west-east routes to and from China, but also the north-south corridors extending through Uzbekistan to and from Afghanistan, the Islamic Republic of Iran, and the Russian Federation. Trade between the border provinces of China and the Central Asian countries happens mostly by road. In particular, Kazakhstan and the Kyrgyz Republic are connected with China by the Almaty-Khorgos-Urumchi road in Kazakhstan and by the Bishkek-Naryn-Torugart-Kashgar and Osh-Sary-Tash-Irkeshtam-Kashgar roads in the Kyrgyz Republic. Tables 4.1 and 4.2 present the volume and value of export and import traffic on the transportation routes to and from China based on recent studies.

Long-distance trade (over 1,000 km) will be implemented by comparatively modern companies operating according to the international standards (for example, Transports Internationaux Routiers [TIR] and Convention on the Contract for the International Carriage of Goods by Road [CMR]). Local cross-border movement on shorter distances (several tens or hundreds of kilometers) is less structured and formal in nature: individual companies with old trucks or bazaar traders transporting their own merchandise. In particular, in the Kyrgyz Republic the wholesale markets play an important role as they function as gateways to reexport Chinese goods to neighboring Central Asian countries and Russia. The value of those reexports and revenues from reexport activities, especially through the channel of wholesale bazaars (Dordoi, Karasuu, and Madina) in the Kyrgyz Republic are reportedly large and increasing. The share of the Dordoi bazaar alone, for example, is estimated to contribute to about one-third of the country's gross domestic product (GDP). These flows concern not only the Ferghana Valley at the intersection between the Kyrgyz Republic, Tajikistan, Uzbekistan, but also Kazakhstan, which was an important destination for Chinese goods going through the Kyrgyz Republic territory until recently.[1] Table 4.3 shows an estimate of the activities at the three main crossing points with China.

**Table 4.1  Import, Export, Transit by Road in Central Asia (Originating in China), 2009**
*Thousand tons*

|  | Kazakhstan | Kyrgyz Republic | Tajikistan | Turkmenistan | Uzbekistan |
|---|---|---|---|---|---|
| Export | 169.2 | 27.9 | 0.5 | n.a. | 45.3 |
| Import | 404.0 | 650.2 | 62.1 | n.a. | 112.0 |
| Transit | 2.4 | 678.1 | 62.6 | 800 | 157.3 |
| Total | 575.6 | 1,356.2 | 125.2 | 2,500 | 314.6 |
| Imports as % of total | 70.2 | 47.9 | 50 | n.a. | 35.6 |
| Transit as % of total | 0.41 | 50 | 50 | 32 | 50 |

*Sources:* IRU 2011a, 2011b.
*Note:* n.a. = not applicable.

**Table 4.2  Export and Import Traffic to and from China, 2011**
*Thousand $*

|  | Export | Import |
|---|---|---|
| Kazakhstan | 16,291,513 | 5,021,098 |
| Kyrgyz Republic | 40,680 | 923,545 |
| Tajikistan | 72,228 | 1,996,778 |

*Source:* UN Comtrade.

**Table 4.3  Volume and Value of Freight Transport through the Main Border Crossings with China, 2011**

|  | Horgos (RK) | Torugart (KR) | Irkeshtam (KR) |
|---|---|---|---|
| Exports and imports, tons | 432,037 | 328,825 | 322,300 |
| Imports, tons | 39.129 | 54,418 | 52,100 |
| General exports, tons | 290,012 | 274,407 | 270,200 |
| Total trade volume, million $ | 1,095.6 | 432.0 | 545.0 |
| Imports, million $ | 64.2 | 41.5 | 33.0 |
| General exports, million $ | 965.4 | 390.5 | 512.0 |

*Source:* Kulipanova 2012.

*Note:* KR = Kyrgyz Republic; RK = Kazakhstan.

## Long-Haul Road Freight Transport and Transports Internationaux Routiers

Although international roads in Central Asia are mostly used for cross-border regional freight, and despite the fact that the rail is the most cost-effective mode for long distances, significant long-haul freight activity is found in Central Asia, mostly under the TIR provision to link the regions with Russia (before the Customs Union) and Europe. Despite the distance, time-sensitive or expensive commodities have a more reliable supply chain by roads. Uzbekistan and Kazakhstan are the most important countries for transit by road and serve the other countries on the Silk Route.

In Uzbekistan, road transit makes up 60 percent of its entire transit transport (894,600 tons). The most heavily used routes run in the north-south direction through Kazakhstan and Turkmenistan (69 percent), with the rest going to/from Tajikistan (21 percent), the Kyrgyz Republic (6 percent), and Afghanistan (4 percent). Uzbekistan is an important transit country for freight bound to Afghanistan; nearly half of Afghanistan's road imports are reported to pass through Hairatan (TRACECA 2010). However, the increase in transit is largely explained by the use of the route to support the North Atlantic Treaty Organization (NATO) operation and to deliver humanitarian assistance, rather than by growing intercontinental trade. Thus, as with railways, international roads are mostly used for regional transport.

A great majority of international shipments outside Central Asia and the Customs Union are transported using TIR carnets for customs transit. TIR trucking is very active in linking Central Asia primarily with Europe, through Russia, as well as Turkey, through the more cumbersome southern corridors. With the Eurasian Customs Union, the TIR is no longer used from and to Russia itself. TIR support is mostly for import, and so their services are largely provided by operators from the partner countries, including the Baltic countries or Turkey. For instance, the share of Kazakhstani trucking companies in the international TIR transit to and from Kazakhstan is about one-third. The Central Asian international trucking industry is thus relatively small compared with that of other countries such as Turkey or Ukraine.

The Eurasian Connection  •  http://dx.doi.org/10.1596/978-0-8213-9912-5

**Table 4.4  Number of Authorized Transports Internationaux Routiers Operators and Carnets Issued to National Associations in Central Asia and in Selected Countries, 2012**

|                    | Number of authorized TIR operators | Number of TIR carnets issued by IRU to national associations |
|--------------------|:---:|:---:|
| Ukraine            | 3,551 | 376,800 |
| Russian Federation | 2,722 | 598,000 |
| Turkey             | 1,622 | 685,000 |
| Belarus            | 1,073 | 215,000 |
| Lithuania          | 888 | 191,600 |
| Latvia             | 504 | 97,800 |
| **Kazakhstan**     | **268** | **19,000** |
| **Uzbekistan**     | **195** | **17,500** |
| Azerbaijan         | 57 | 11,400 |
| **Kyrgyz Republic**| **83** | **17,100** |
| Armenia            | 55 | 3,800 |

*Sources:* http://www.unece.org/tir/figures/tir-figures-authoriz.html; http://www.unece.org/fileadmin/DAM/tir/figures/TIRCarnets12.pdf.
*Note:* Bold values are data for Central Asian countries.

Presently, alternative ways of providing customs guarantees are very rarely used. In the territory of the Customs Union, controls are no longer conducted, and the border with Belarus and Russia (except for passport control) and TIR, or any other guarantee form, is no longer needed in intra–Customs Union transportation. According to the United Nations Economic Commission for Europe (UNECE) Transport Division, the number of TIR carnets issued by the International Road Union for Kazakhstan decreased from 30,500 in 2010 to 19,000 in 2012 (table 4.4).[2]

Recently (mid-2013), the problem of compatibility between the TIR and the transit regime within the Customs Union has been raised by the Russian authorities. This created some concerns regarding the future of transit supply chains originating from Europe under the TIR. In Europe the common transit regime to the EU and European Free Trade Association (EFTA) countries includes provisions that spell out the continuity between the TIR and common transit. Implementation of the transit regime in the Eurasian Customs Union may follow the same principle (see chapters 6 and 7).

The documentation for international road freight transport follows international practices. The required documents are an international CMR waybill, commercial invoice, TIR carnet, and possibly other certificates. The Convention on International Transport of Goods under Cover of TIR Carnets (TIR Convention) was agreed to in Geneva on November 14, 1975, to simplify and harmonize the administrative formalities of international road transport. The TIR system once was very important in Western Europe, but after the establishment of the EU and the breakup of the Soviet Union, it moved to the east. Currently it is used for international transport between the EU and non-EU European countries, Commonwealth of Independent States countries, the Islamic Republic of Iran, and Turkey. The TIR system allows a carrier to collect cargo from three different loading points and to deliver cargo to three different destinations.

## Framework of International Road Freight Transport and Transit along the Silk Road

Recent research (Arvis 2010) shows that transportation costs alone do not account for trade costs along transport routes. It is important to take into account other important outcomes in supply-chain performance, such as delays, reliability, or service quality, all of which depend on what could be referred to as the transit system. The "transit system" refers to the infrastructure, legal framework, institutions, and procedures serving truckers (see figure 4.1). The performance of the various components of this system explains in large part the outcome in trade and supply-chain connectivity in the region. The importance of those components and their weaknesses in the context of Central Asian conditions is reviewed in more detail in chapter 6.

**Figure 4.1  Components of the Transit System**

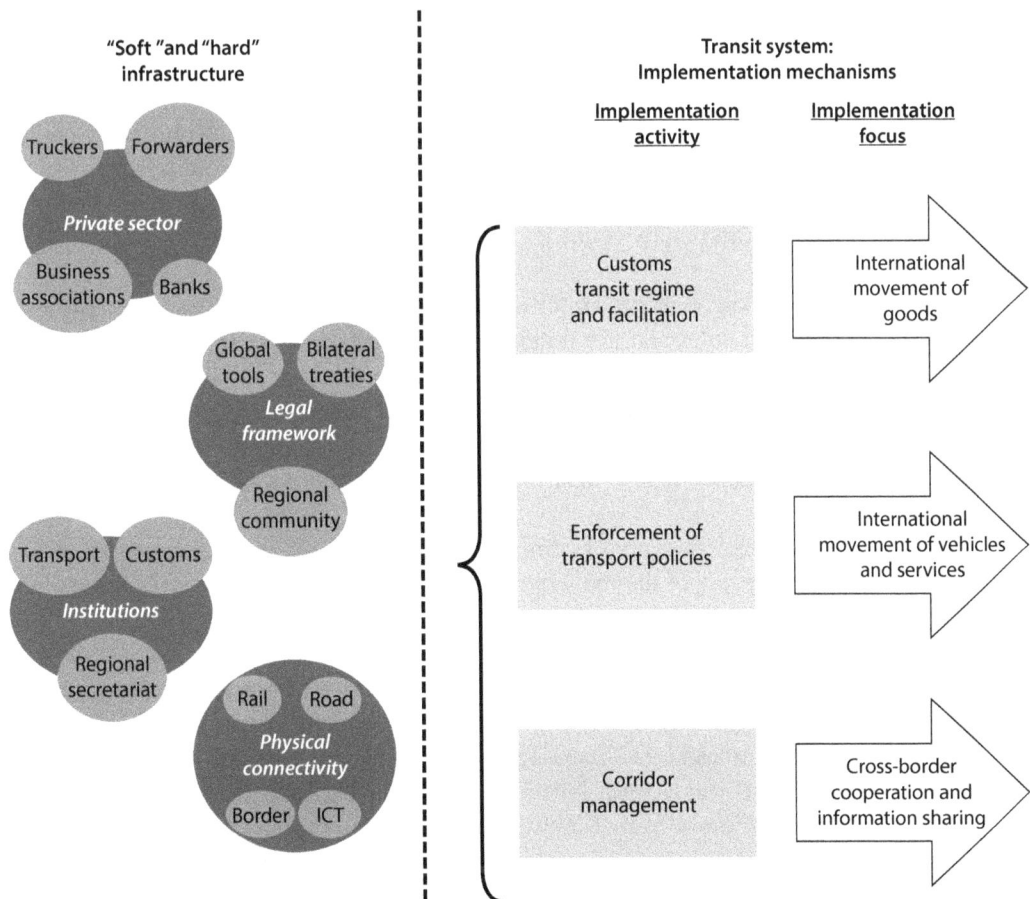

The first order of components corresponds to the hard and soft infrastructure of trade and transportation. The provision of physical connections through road and rail links is an obvious requirement. It concerns not merely transportation links, but also border-crossing facilities. Service markets, including trucking, customs brokers, and freight forwarders, are available in the region but are less developed. Efficient public sector institutions that are in charge of the enforcement of rules and the facilitation of transportation and trade include customs, port authorities in transit countries, road agencies in both countries (enforcement of axle load), and road transportation regulators. The efficiencies of these institutions is reviewed in chapter 7.

The international legal framework is essential to the soft infrastructure of trade routes (box 4.1). It comprises three levels:

- Global conventions that set commonly accepted principles in areas such as customs (such as the Kyoto convention) and transit (the TIR convention). Just by adhering to the principles of those conventions, countries and their transit countries will meet a minimal but efficient set of standards in their own procedures and the regulation of the underlying services.

- Overall, the republics of Central Asia, apart from Turkmenistan, have committed to the multilateral framework, especially the convention tied to the UNECE of which the countries have been consistently active members (see box 4.1, table B4.1.1). Even if in the end it results from a country-by-country approach, the principle of adoption of these instruments results from a regional action plan that should also facilitate access to international expertise for the implementation by countries in the region.

- Regional agreements are critical to harmonize processes such as customs or transport rules and are potentially the most effective in facilitating regional trade and transportation. Regional agreements have all but disappeared since the Soviet era. New regional cooperation concepts are just reemerging. For instance, the Eurasian Customs Union, which comprises Kazakhstan and Russia (in addition to Belarus), provides a common customs code.

The second category of components is institutions and implementation tools that make possible the movement of vehicles and loads along international road and rail links in the region:

- A transit regime, implemented mostly by customs agencies, comprising the operating procedures that govern the movement of goods (box 4.2). Long-distance transit is facilitated by the TIR regime or the Customs Union code for Kazakhstan and Russia. No regional system will, for instance, allow a single procedure to move from Tajikistan to Kazakhstan through the Kyrgyz Republic.
- Transport policies and protocols, which govern the movement of vehicles. They are implemented in countries and across borders to regulate logistics

## Box 4.1 The Utilization of International Instruments

Global conventions typically provide a minimally consistent set of implementation principles that a country can use to trade with distant countries or with its neighbors. However, these conventions do not substitute for deeper regional integration that covers a greater area in more depth, such as is the case of the Eurasian Customs Union, where a common customs code is available and common transport policies have been designed.

The principal international conventions relating to international trade facilitation, notably within the regional framework of transit by land, are the following:

- The TIR convention, which is the most widely used system for international road transport; it allows the movement of freight in customs transit through several countries (1975).
- The CR convention, which covers contracts for international road freight transport (Geneva, 1956).
- The ATP convention, which governs the international transport of perishable foodstuffs and special vehicles (September 1, 1970).
- The International Convention on the Simplification and Harmonization of Customs Procedures, or Kyoto convention (revised in 1999).
- The Geneva convention on harmonization of goods control at borders (1982).
- The convention on road traffic (1968).
- The convention on traffic signaling (1968).
- The agreement relative to international transport of dangerous goods by road (1957).
- The customs convention relative to the temporary import of commercial road vehicles (1956).

This list is inspired by the list of conventions deemed essential by the United Nations Economic and Social Commission for Asia and the Pacific (UNESCAP), in its resolution 48/11 of 1992.

**Table B4.1.1  Participation of Central Asian Countries in Conventions and Organizations Facilitating Trade and Transportation**

| Conventions or organization | Kazakhstan | Kyrgyz Republic | Tajikistan | Turkmenistan | Uzbekistan |
|---|---|---|---|---|---|
| TIR | Yes | Yes | Yes | Yes | Yes |
| Kyoto | Yes | No | No | No | No |
| CMR | Yes | Yes | Yes | Yes | Yes |
| ATP | Yes | Yes | Yes | No | Yes |
| Road traffic | Yes | Yes | Yes | Yes | Yes |
| ADR dangerous goods | Yes | No | Yes | No | No |
| World Trade Organization | No | Yes | Yes | No | No |
| Eurasian Customs Union | Yes | No | No | No | No |

The Eurasian Connection • http://dx.doi.org/10.1596/978-0-8213-9912-5

---

**Box 4.2  Transit Regime**

The cornerstone of long-distance transit trade is the customs transit regime. The transit regime is the set of procedures under which goods are transported through countries from one customs operation to another without payment of duties, domestic consumption taxes, or other charges normally due on imports and exports. Transit happens in sealed vehicles and against a form of guarantee issued by the principal of the transit operation (freight forwarder and/or transportation company). Customs at the point of entry expedites the goods in transit with simplified procedures, as compared with clearance for domestic consumption. The role of the guarantee is to cover the fiscal risk of fraud in which goods would "leak" in the country of transit. This concern may be very serious with transport operators and traders who are not very compliant and explains why in many countries transit is not facilitated.

Another efficiency concern is the possibility of integrating transit procedures across all countries. In the context of a customs union such as the European Union, and now the Eurasian Customs Union (Belarus, Kazakhstan, and Russia), this is a simple matter, because there is only one transit operation of the unified customs territory. The matter is more complex where separate customs territories are found. The Transports Internationaux Routiers (TIR) transit regime to which the regional countries are parties (with the exception of China) provides the default solution for long-distance trade by road. The TIR is a global system managed by the United Nations Economic Commission for Europe (UNECE) and implemented by the International Road Transport Union (IRU). The TIR does not posit a regional harmonized framework for trade, customs, and transportation, but rather assumes chained transit activities across borders with a common customs guarantee managed by the IRU. The TIR is also tied to common standards for transport operators and vehicles.

---

services, to recover infrastructure costs, and to improve competition within and between modes of transportation.

• Corridor management institutions or the survey of corridor performance indicators for common solutions. Several corridor initiatives exist in the Central Asia region (see appendix A).

The potential for conflict between the TIR and the new Customs Union transit does exist and should be addressed. In 2013 Russia unilaterally imposed additional requirements for TIR transit on its territory, in the form of additional guarantees. Such a move has spurred a dispute with the EU parties to the TIR convention.

## Notes

1. One of the reasons was arguably the higher import tariffs and higher costs at the Kazakh border-crossing points. The situation has changed because of border closures related to the events in the Kyrgyz Republic in 2010 and as a result of the Customs Union with Belarus and Russia.

2. http://www.unece.org/fileadmin/DAM/tir/figures/TIRCarnets12.pdf.

## References

Arvis, Jean-François. 2010. *The Cost of Being Landlocked: Logistics Costs and Supply Chain Reliability*. Directions in Development 558837. Washington, DC: World Bank.

IRU (International Road Union). 2011a. "Analysis of Traffic Flow in Central Asia and Border Areas of China." ("Анализ грузопотоков в Центральной Азии и приграничных районов Китая.") Moscow. http://www.iru-nelti.org/index/ru_publications.

———. 2011b. "An Analysis of Goods Flow in Central Asia and Border Regions of China, Executive Summary." Moscow. http://www.iru-nelti.org/index/en_publications.

Kulipanova, Elena. 2012. "International Transport in Central Asia: Understanding the Patterns of (Non)-Cooperation." Working Paper 2, University of Central Asia, Bishkek.

TRACECA. 2010. *International Logistics Centres/Nodes Network Central Asia at the Republic of Kazakhstan, Kyrgyz Republic, Republic of Tajikistan, Republic of Uzbekistan and the Republic of Turkmenistan, Task A Report, Reissued July 15 2010*. European Union, Brussels.

# CHAPTER 5

# Supply-Chain Efficiency and Logistics Costs

This chapter reviews the evidence on supply-chain performance and logistics costs on the modern Silk Route. It is based on information from the railway industry, corridor surveys by various organizations, trip diaries, and data and interviews from trucking companies, traders, and manufacturers.

Although the unit transportation costs may not be high, many factors increase delays and reduce the reliability of the supply-chain connection of traders in Central Asia and increase the burden of logistics costs on commerce.

## Logistics and Supply-Chain Efficiency

Supply chains are the backbone of economic activities and support production, commerce, and international trade. Logistics or supply-chain management administers various activities on the supply chain, which typically include, for example, freight transportation, warehousing, transloading or transhipment, customs clearance, and customs transit.

Most experts agree that the performance of a supply chain should be assessed from the perspective of the user. For instance, most global supply chains are organized by and for international companies. The choice of logistics solutions, including routes or mode of transportation, is the responsibility of these supply-chain principals, although some aspects may be delegated to their logistics providers. These choices are idiosyncratic and depend on their own expectations of the level of supply performance and their own benchmarks for delivery of goods along the supply chain. The choice among alternatives, including modes of transportation, is therefore driven by demand and results from arbitrage between several parameters.

At the microeconomic level and from a user perspective, the primary dimensions in supply-chain performance include cost (fees paid for services such as transportation and administration), time (the average lead time to move goods along the chain), and reliability (the delivery of goods on schedule). An additional attribute closely linked with reliability is the flexibility or resilience of the supply chain. It is an ability to employ alternative solutions in case the main chain is interrupted. It means, for instance, being able to find trucks when train services are not available in the desired time frame.

Reliability is subjective and more difficult to measure. One way to measure reliability is to look at the variability, or probability distribution, of the lead time. It has been found recently that typical distributions of lead time on land corridors and ports have an asymmetric shape with long tails (Arvis 2010). The consequence is that a consignee may have to cope with a situation in which the goods to be used in the supply chain will not arrive on time. Unreliability mainly arises when the goods are not in movement, for instance, in the context of Kazakhstan:

- Variance in time it takes to clear goods at destination.
- Control en route of trucks in Kazakhstan or the Russian Federation.
- Wagons not moving because they are waiting in a marshaling yard to be dispatched to the final consignee.
- Delays caused by weather.

Reliability is subjective in the sense that it depends on the specifics of a given supply chain, including the type of industry and product exchange (figure 5.1).

**Figure 5.1  Logistics and Supply-Chain Efficiency: Reliability versus Costs**

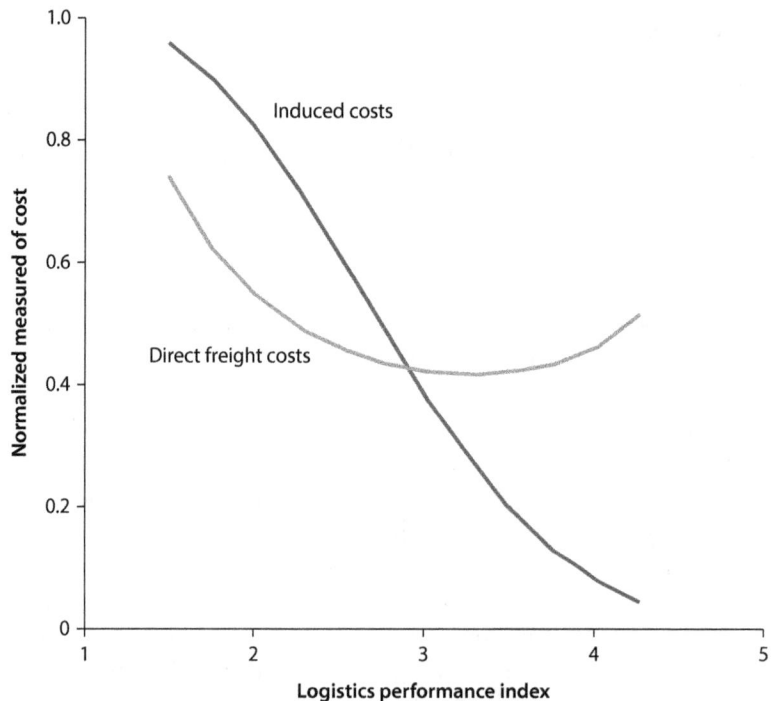

*Source:* World Bank 2007.

**Table 5.1 The Three Components of Total Logistics Costs**

| C = | (1) Transportation costs = | Fees paid for actual transit transportation services to truckers or rail operators[a] |
|---|---|---|
| + | (2) Other logistics costs = | (a) Transit overhead; fees, procedures, facilitation payments + (b) Fixed costs of shipments |
| + | (3) Delayed hedging costs = | (a) In-transit moving inventory costs (costs of goods maintained on the road while already paid for, for example, cost of average transit time) + (b) Induced costs to hedge unreliability plus inventory and warehousing costs or to shift to a faster, more expensive mode of transportation |

*Source:* Arvis 2010.

a. Transportation costs include transportation fees, and logistics costs include overhead and inventories costs.

For instance, variance in lead time, under normal circumstances, has little impact on chains for bulk commodities. These commodities, such as coal or grain, are stored at both origin and destination and thus can be transported with cheaper but less reliable modes of transportation. By contrast, as a part of international manufacturing supply chains, delivery is expected to have well-defined windows so as not to disrupt the supply chain. A relatively small tolerance for delays is encountered—one or two days—even though the total transportation time may be in weeks, as in the case of Euro-Asian trade. International logistics providers in the business of moving time-sensitive goods closely follow key performance indicators of service delivery (delivery within the agreed schedule).

What makes Central Asian countries, as well as other developing countries, stand apart is the very low reliability of their supply chains. The probability of something going wrong en route is high: containers held up for controls, breakdown of equipment, or even stolen cargo. The processes and activity in the supply chain are themselves quite unpredictable. An average delay does not mean much, because, in fact, the distribution of delays is very wide, with a high probability of delays largely exceeding the average by a large margin (table 5.1).[1]

## Performance of Transcontinental Rail Transit: Europe-Asia

To analyze the cost of shipping containers from China through these routes (figure 5.2), railway tariffs for three competing routes were developed: (1) from Zabaikalsk (on the Russia-China border in the far east) to St. Petersburg, (2) from Naushki (at the Mongolian border with Russia) to St. Petersburg, and (3) from Dostyk (the major gateway between Kazakhstan and China) to St. Petersburg or from Khorgos (Altynkol) to St. Petersburg. For two of the routes prices for November 2011 and February 2013 were developed; the Khorgos route was opened in late 2012, so tariffs for this route are only for 2013.

The analysis shows that the use of private wagons generally is cheapest, but the charges that are computed in this analysis do not include empty movements—the assumption being that there would be a container to pick up in St. Petersburg's container port to go somewhere else and there would not be an empty return movement. This analysis estimates the cost of using private wagons and private containers (as opposed to railway inventory containers and wagons), and the wagon cost is divided between two containers in all private wagon cases.

Three gateways are shown in figure 5.2:

- Dostyk, Kazakhstan; the tariffs include both Kazakhstan Temir Jolu (KTZ) and Russian Railways (RZD) charges.
- Naushki, on the Mongolian border with Russia; the tariffs do not include the Mongolian Railway charges.
- Zabaikalsk, on the Russia-China border in far northern China.

None of the tariffs include charges by China, freight forwarders, or terminal charges; they include only the railway tariff and equipment costs. The results show that transport costs for container movements through Kazakhstan are the most expensive, averaging above $7,000 per container. It should be expected that these differences will equalize as the Customs Union begins to standardize transit tariffs. The high transportation rates through Kazakhstan may lead to an increased use of alternative routes.

**Figure 5.2  Rail Costs for 40-Foot Container in Transit**

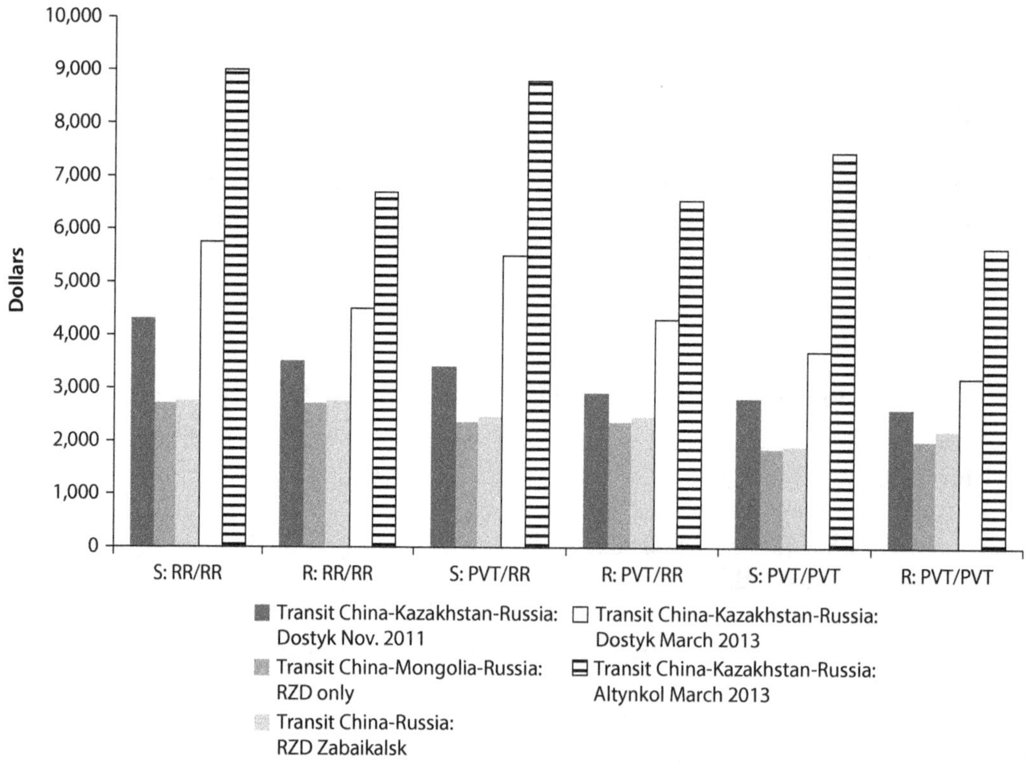

Legend:
- Transit China-Kazakhstan-Russia: Dostyk Nov. 2011
- Transit China-Kazakhstan-Russia: Dostyk March 2013
- Transit China-Mongolia-Russia: RZD only
- Transit China-Kazakhstan-Russia: Altynkol March 2013
- Transit China-Russia: RZD Zabaikalsk

*Note:* S: Special high-speed block train; R: Regular manifest freight train; RR/RR: Railway container/Railway wagon; PVT/RR: Private container/Railway wagon; PVT/PVT: Private container, private wagon.

Rail transport has a clear, natural cost advantage over road transportation for a given distance, as well as greater reliability, for transcontinental freight.

Rail transport encounters fewer delay activities than road transport, but the most frequent causes for delays are generally more time-consuming in rail transport (change of gauge or classification of trains' waiting time in queue), for example, 29.6 hours in waiting when transporting by rail versus 5.5 hours in waiting when transporting by road (see appendix D). Securities services, clearance fees, and loading and unloading are the main cost contributors (Central Asia Regional Economic Cooperation [CAREC], CPMM 2011 study on six CAREC corridors).

Although many studies indicate that rail transport could be faster than maritime transport for transcontinental transit container trains, evidence from interviews with traders and freight forwarders undertaken as part of this analysis shows that lead times are reportedly high, and reliability low. Additionally, obsolete railway infrastructure and rolling stock in central Asia, considerably slow the train speed on the rail network (the average freight train speed in Kazakhstan in 2009 was only 41.9 kilometers per hour [km/h], whereas the rail speed along the six CAREC corridors averages 11–38 km/h).

However, the main constraint seems to be the unpredictability of the time of arrival of wagons and containers due to the lack of a precise transit schedule, as well as of the transfer or marshaling of individual wagons and containers (figure 5.3). The authors interviewed traders who mentioned that containers are sometimes lost for weeks, especially those coming from China.

Scenarios on travel time and cost for block trains along the Trans-Kazakhstan Railways (TKR) present significant time savings. Container trains that cover the distance from eastern China ports to Western European logistics centers take about two weeks, which is a very competitive transit time compared with the 40 days by maritime transport.

A comparison of market prices for block trains with single-wagon loads shows a clear advantage for block trains in terms of cost and time, which can

**Figure 5.3  High Wear and Tear of Rolling Stock in Kazakhstan, 2009**

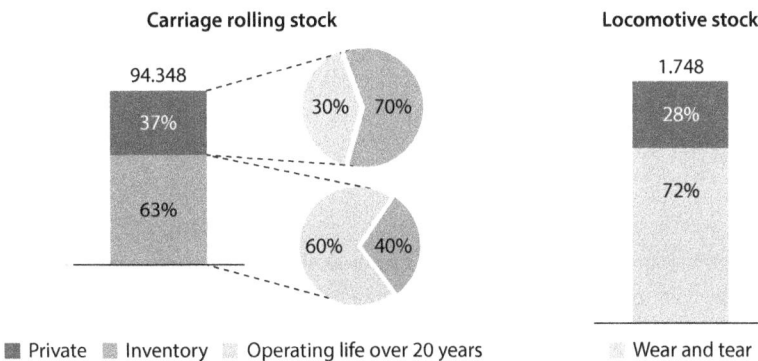

Carriage rolling stock

94.348

37%

63%

30%  70%

60%  40%

Locomotive stock

1.748

28%

72%

■ Private   ■ Inventory   Operating life over 20 years          Wear and tear

*Source:* AECOM 2011.

**Table 5.2  Lead Time and Cost for Container Block Trains on TKR and TSR**

| Route: Duisburg-Lanzhou | Trans-Kazakhstan | Transsiberian (Mongolian) | Transsiberian (Manchurian) |
|---|---|---|---|
| Distance, km | 9,118 | 12,028 | 13,055 |
| Lead time (days) | | | |
| Single wagon | 28 | 38 | 39 |
| Container block trains | 18 | 22 | 22 |
| Cost ($) | | | |
| Single wagon | 6,730 | 6,705 | 6,705 |
| Container block trains | 3,200 | 4,700 | 4,600 |

*Source:* European Commission 2012.

be explained by discounts on booking block trains or other factors such as the employment of private wagons (table 5.2).[2]

## Performance of Long-Distance Road Transportation: Turkey–Central Asia and Uzbekistan–Russia

Moving freight by truck continues to be time-consuming and expensive, mainly because of lengthy customs clearance procedures, loading and unloading for road and rail transport, unofficial payments, and change in rail gauge. Evidence from studies of the time and cost to transit Central Asian countries and cross land borders indicates that formal procedures make up less than half of the average total transit time, the remainder being spent waiting in queue and transloading as well as changing rail gauge (see appendix D).

On average, it takes almost 12 hours for a truck to get across a land border in Central Asia, significantly longer than at comparable crossings in other regions. Border-crossing activities tend to add 50 percent to the time to transit a corridor and increase cost in most corridors. In response to the many efforts the Asian Development Bank (CAREC, CPMM) has made to reduce land border-crossing times, there has been a consistent reduction since 2009, totaling 20 percent in the average and 7 percent in the median times. This can be explained partly by the impacts of the creation of the Customs Union, but also by improvements made at some border crossings not affected by this change.

However, lead time is highly variable, which indicates that no guarantee can be given on the overall transit time. It costs $700–1,750 to move 20 tons of cargo over 500 km in Central Asia, of which border crossings make up 40–70 percent of the cost. Transloading and queuing at the border is a time-consuming and costly activity, but inspections by the state automobile inspectorate (GAI) are reportedly contributing to high road freight rates as well. The coefficient of variation of transit time requires more investigation; as for shippers, freight arrival reliability is a major factor in deciding which corridors and mode of transport to use.

An analysis of data collected from trip diaries in 2010–11 by the associations of the International Road Transport Union (IRU) on the corridors linking

Central Asian countries to Europe shows that truck traffic is characterized by the following:

- Significant variability in speed across countries and within countries, as measured, for instance, by the average distance per day and its coefficient of variation (figure 5.4).
- A high level of additional costs paid on top of transportation services to keep the trucks moving, including unofficial payments, up to 30 cents per km when the cost of transportation itself is in the range of $1.00–1.50 per km (table 5.3).

The performance tends to be better for long-distance transit and better on the northern routes through Russia than on the southern routes to the Black Sea (the Islamic Republic of Iran, Turkey, and the Caucasus).

These additional (informal) costs may vary depending on the route and, unfortunately, with identified corrupt practices. Collusion between customs staff and customs brokers may have led in certain instances to a much higher level of corruption. In 2011–12 it was reported that traders had to pay up to $14,000 in the peak season for transportation of a full load of 86 cubic meters from Khorgos (Kazakhstan-China border) to Almaty, a distance of 350 km. The most plausible

**Table 5.3  Additional Costs Paid by Truckers on Southern Corridors from Central Asia to Turkey**

*Dollars per kilometer*

|  | *Formal costs* | *Informal costs* |
|---|---|---|
| Cross-border | 0.32 | 0.09 |
| Transit | 0.13 | 0.07 |

*Source:* IRU trip diaries.

**Figure 5.4  Median Speed and Reliability for Transit Country, All Corridors**

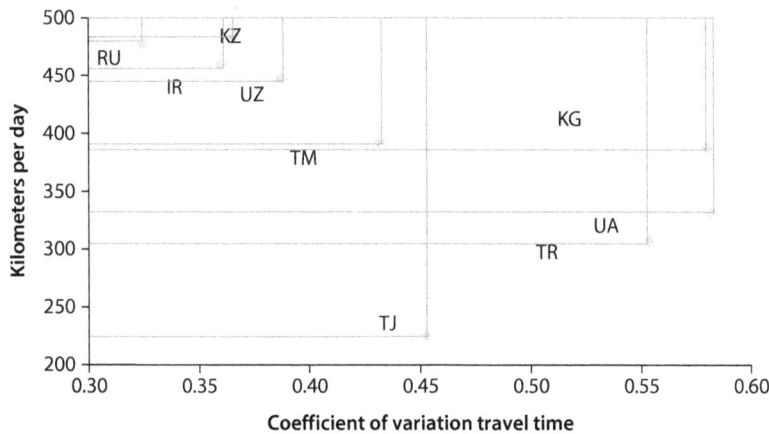

*Source:* IRU trip diaries.
*Note:* IR = Iran, KG = Kyrgyz Republic, KZ = Kazakhstan, RU = Russia, TJ = Tajikistan, TR = Turkey, TM = Turkmenistan, UA = Ukraine, and UZ = Uzbekistan.

The Eurasian Connection • http://dx.doi.org/10.1596/978-0-8213-9912-5

explanation was a criminal ring—subsequently discovered and dismantled—at the border where trucks and traders had to pay a large informal amount to import.

The background survey and interviews prepared as part of this analysis evidenced the operational efficiency of trucking services. The use of equipment is fairly inefficient, which is one of the reasons for poor competitiveness. For example, a respondent company in the Kyrgyz Republic with 75 trucks makes six or seven trips to Europe (30 percent) and Russia (70 percent) per month. Round trips to Europe take 30 days, and trips to Russia take 22 days approximately. An average truck makes trips about 160 days of the year. Of these, 45 days are spent on idle standing. Carriers spend long times at places of origin and places of destination. When hauling to Western Europe, for example, the actual transportation time of a round trip is 20 days, and the time spent on idle standing is about 10 days. Overall, trucks are in effective use only about one-third of the time.

Few of the respondent companies use real-time monitoring of trucks other than mobile phones. GPS tracking equipment and other advanced solutions are considered too expensive. Nor are advanced computer systems in use apart from regular personal computers. On the other hand, carriers do use web-based marketplaces such as Della.com extensively to find loads. These portals serve carriers well. They increase profitability, lowering the costs of sales by increasing the possibility of finding backloads.

As is the case for rail transportation, road freight rates (charges to the shippers) are highly influenced by numerous variable costs (truck utilization, fuel prices, and other expenses). The share of fuel cost in total operating costs seems to be comparatively high in Central Asia (30–35 percent). The cost structure shown in figure 5.5 has been obtained from companies through surveys and interviews.

**Figure 5.5  Cost Structure of Four Companies Transporting by Road in Kazakhstan**
*Percent*

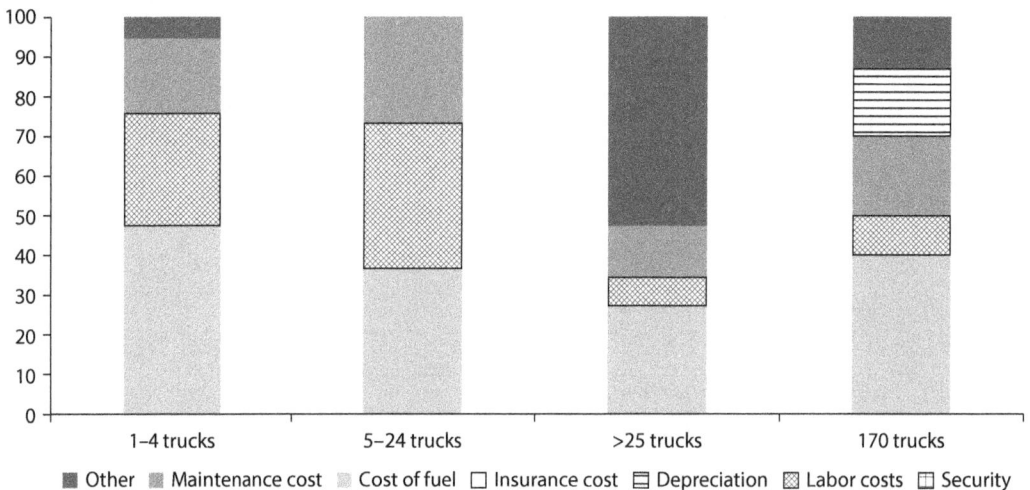

Legend: ■ Other  ▨ Maintenance cost  ▨ Cost of fuel  □ Insurance cost  ▤ Depreciation  ▧ Labor costs  ⊞ Security

*Sources:* IRU 2006; survey and expert interviews.

Because the number of companies responding to the question on the structure of their costs was quite small, it is hard to draw solid conclusions. But it can be said that the costs vary depending on the size of the trucking company. Smaller companies that own one to four trucks tend to have a higher percentage of labor and maintenance costs. The larger companies (more than 25 trucks) report large expenses for other costs. Figure 5.6 provides a cost structure for select European and the Kyrgyz Republic carriers. Labor and fuel costs in Kazakhstan seem to be on par with similar costs in Europe and the Kyrgyz Republic.

According to a recent survey undertaken for this analysis, most carriers have to run empty one-third to one-half of a trip to have access to profitable import loads.

In Kazakhstan, for example, collected sample freight prices for shipments to Russia and Germany are only 53 percent of import prices from those countries (figures 5.7 and 5.8).

A likely reason for the great variation of import prices is that carriers often set "ad hoc" prices based on whether or not they have both transport "legs" loaded.

Data from the Central Asian road freight transport market indicate that traders in Tajikistan pay significantly more for road haulage than traders in Kazakhstan because of the existence of a more mature market. In the import market, rates measured in ton-km are somewhat on the same level as in the Customs Union, other Commonwealth of Independent States countries, and Europe (varying from 7.0 to 7.4 cents/ton-km) (see appendix E).

**Figure 5.6  Cost Structure of Road Carriage in Europe and for Four Kyrgyz Carriers**
*Percent*

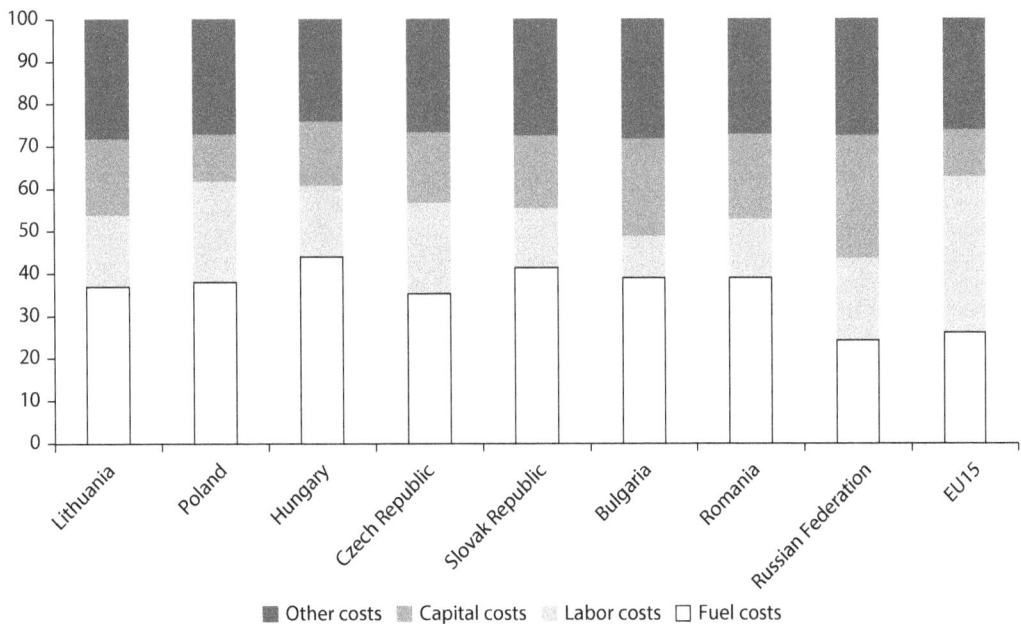

■ Other costs    ▨ Capital costs    ░ Labor costs    □ Fuel costs

*figure continues next page*

**Figure 5.6  Cost Structure of Road Carriage in Europe and for Four Kyrgyz Carriers** *(continued)*

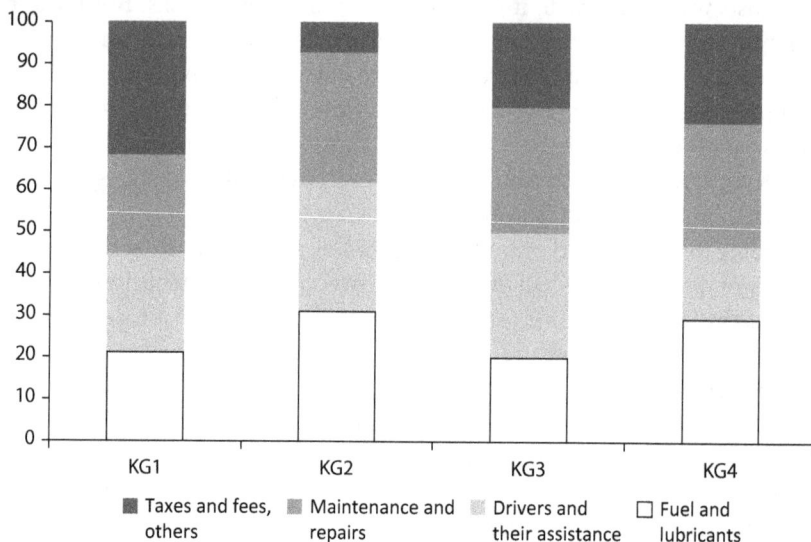

Legend:
- Taxes and fees, others
- Maintenance and repairs
- Drivers and their assistance
- Fuel and lubricants

*Sources:* IRU 2006; expert interviews.

**Figure 5.7  Prices for Freight Transportation from/to Russia to/from Kazakhstan (as of April 2013)**

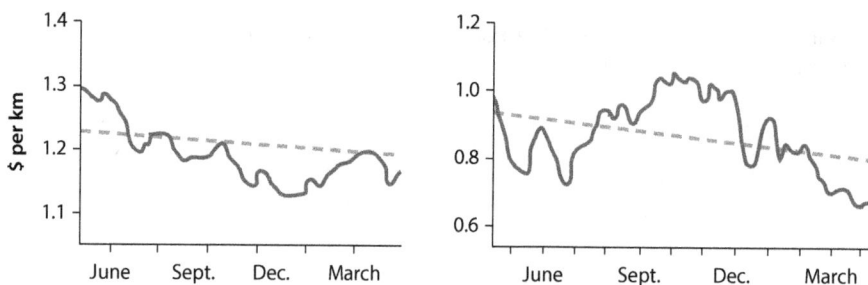

*Source:* www.tm-della.com.

**Figure 5.8  Prices for Freight Transportation from/to Germany to/from Kazakhstan (as of April 2013)**

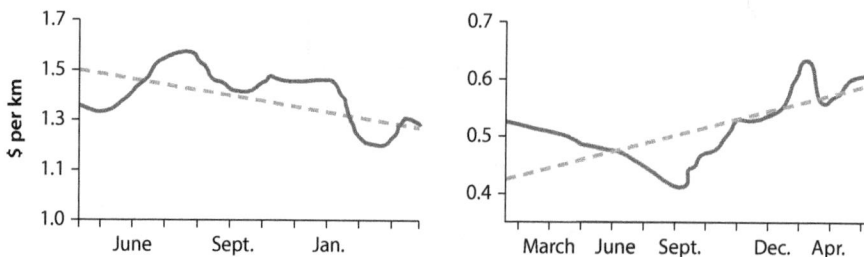

*Source:* www.tm-della.com.

Another measure of transportation costs is the cost of traction of a semitrailer per km, averaging empty and full trips. The cost of traction was in early 2013 about $1 per km for both international and long-distance transportation within the Customs Union (Kazakhstan and Russia). This value is in the lower range of international comparisons (lower than Europe and at par with South Africa or the United States).

## Impact of Supply-Chain Inefficiencies: Logistics Costs

An alternative way of looking at the supply-chain constraints for the Central Asian countries along the Silk Route is to compare the share of logistics with the turnover and value added of wholesale and manufacturing activities. Figure 5.9 shows an example of logistics costs in manufacturing and trading companies in an EU country. The costs are measured as a percentage of net sales.

In Central Asia, most of the companies interviewed in Kazakhstan report challenging operating conditions with long replenishment cycles and big inventories. Total reaction time to resupply is two months, typically including 40 days in transit from plants in Russia or Europe. A wholesaler maintains two to three

**Figure 5.9  Logistics Costs Broken into Components as a Percentage of Net Sales: Example of Finland**

*Percent*

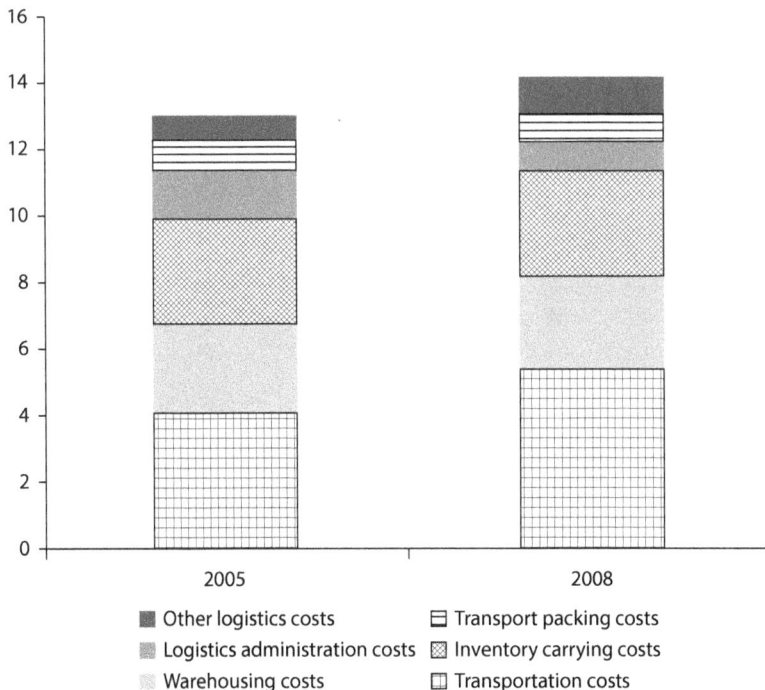

Source: Solakivi et al. 2009.
Note: Survey data from 1,291 firms.

The Eurasian Connection • http://dx.doi.org/10.1596/978-0-8213-9912-5

months' stocks in warehouses (for nonperishable products). This level of inventory is much higher than in Europe and the United States (a couple of weeks), and about the same as is found in other landlocked countries, including in the southern Africa region.

Losses reported by companies are a very significant 3 percent in wholesale activities (figure 5.10). Losses happen in transit because of the condition of transportation. Furthermore, theft seems a major concern in Belarus and western Kazakhstan. Adding all the sources of logistics costs implies that their total is a high proportion of turnover in commercial activities (table 5.4), at least double what they are in a member country of the Organisation for Economic Co-operation and Development (10–12 percent).

**Figure 5.10  Total Logistics Costs versus Transportation Costs**

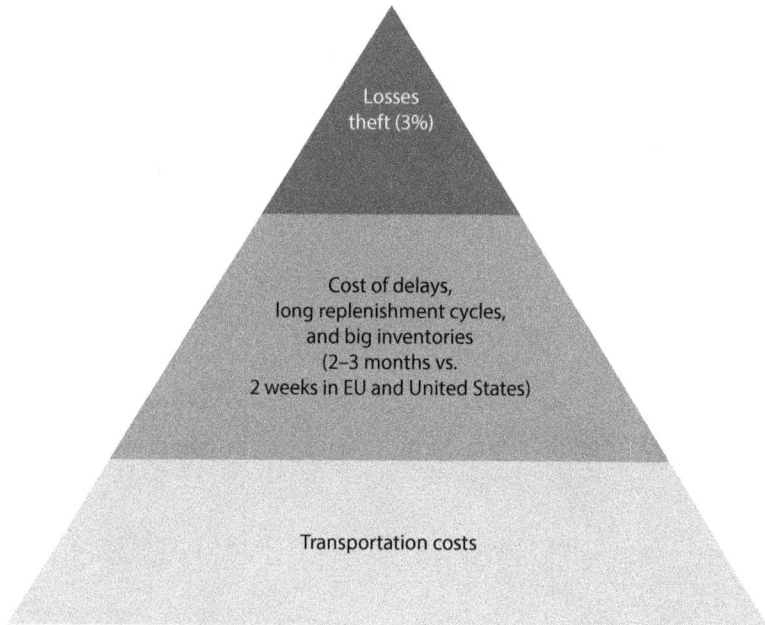

**Table 5.4  Total Logistics Costs in Retail Activity in Kazakhstan**
*Percent*

| Transportation | 7 | Interview |
|---|---|---|
| Certification | 2 | Interview |
| Inventory | 5 | 40 days in transit and two months inventory at 0.05% per day |
| Losses | 3 | Interview |
| Other administration | 5 | Authors' estimate |
| Total logistics costs | 22 | |

Other estimates concur that logistics costs for imports in Central Asia are much in excess of what is observed in Europe or the United States. According to an estimate made as part of this report, logistics costs for Kazakhstan, the Kyrgyz Republic, and Tajikistan are estimated to be 18–23 percent of exported value and 16–18 percent of imported value (table 5.5). According to an estimate by the Asian Development Bank (2006), transport costs account for 10 percent of the export trade value and 8 percent of the import trade in Kazakhstan. Ojala (2005) estimates other export/import-related logistics costs in the Central Asia region at generally 7–10 percent of exported value and 5–8 percent of imported value.

The cost level is very high in an international comparison. For example, transport costs accounted for 8.4 percent of the import value in Asia as a whole and only 6.1 percent of the total value of imports in the world. High logistics costs are impacting the potential of export and diversification because they raise the costs of inputs and the costs of exports. A 2013 survey of exporters shows that they are even more impacted by logistics costs than importers (table 5.6).

Improvement in performance not only would boost the new Silk Route transit, but would also unlock the potential for more regional trade.

**Table 5.5  Estimates of Logistics Costs of Trading in Central Asia**
*Percent*

|  |  | Kyrgyz Republic | Kazakhstan | Tajikistan |
|---|---|---|---|---|
| Transportation cost | Export | 13 | 10 | 14 |
|  | Import | 10 | 8 | 10 |
| Other logistics cost | Export | 7–10 | 7–10 | 7–10 |
|  | Import | 5–8 | 5–8 | 5–8 |
| Total logistics cost | Export | 20–23 | 17–20 | 21–24 |
|  | Import | 15–18 | 13–16 | 15–18 |
| Total logistics cost used in this report | Export | 20 | 18 | 23 |
|  | Import | 17 | 16 | 18 |

*Source:* World Bank 2013.

**Table 5.6  Percentage of Turnover Allocated to Logistics Costs**

| | |
|---|---|
| Transportation and cargo handling (including transport packaging) | 11.09 |
| Warehousing (cost of running own warehouse or renting one) | 2.86 |
| Inventory carrying cost (including cost of capital tied up in inventory) | 27.67 |
| Logistics administration (costs from functions indirectly related to logistics) | 6.00 |
| All other logistics costs | 9.88 |

*Sources:* Survey of Exporters Kazinvest 2013.

## Notes

1. For a typical distribution of delays, 10 percent of the delays will exceed 200 percent of the average, and 5 percent of them will exceed 300 percent.

2. It should be noted that according to the official railway tariff policy, a discount of 10 percent on the freight rates for single-wagon loads is given in the case of booking block trains. Other factors influencing the actual market price are the employment of private wagons (at a 15 percent discount) and further rebates depending on volume and fees for coordination and administration (European Commission 2012).

## References

AECOM. 2011. *Transport and Logistics Strategy of the Republic of Kazakhstan till 2030.* Astana.

Arvis, Jean-François. 2010. *The Cost of Being Landlocked: Logistics Costs and Supply Chain Reliability.* Directions in Development 558837. Washington, DC: World Bank.

European Commission. 2012. *Potential for Eurasia Land Bridge Corridors & Logistics Developments along the Corridors.* Brussels.

IRU (International Road Transport Union). 2006. *Selected Recent Statistics on Road Freight Transport in Europe.* http://www.iru.org/cms-filesystem-action?file=mix-publications /statistics_Goods.pdf.

Ojala, Lauri. 2005. "Analysis of Transport Issues: Study on Central Asia Regional Cooperation in Trade, Transport, and Transit." Seminar presentation, Almaty, June 10–11.

Solakivi, Tomi, Lauri Ojala, Juuso Toyli, Hanne-Mari Halinen, Harri Lorrentz, Karri Rantasila, and Tapio Naula. 2009. *Finland—State of Logistics 2009.* Helsinki: Ministry of Transport and Communications.

World Bank. 2007. *Connecting to Compete: Trade Logistics in the Global Economy.* World Bank, Washington, DC.

———. 2013. *Road Transport and Logistics Providers in Central Asia: Kazakhstan, Kyrgyz Republic and Tajikistan.* World Bank, Washington, DC.

CHAPTER 6

# Underlying Obstacles to Supply-Chain Efficiency

This chapter reviews the main institutional, organizational, and behavioral factors explaining the performance of supply chains connecting the countries in Central Asia. It reviews the sources of low performance in logistics bottlenecks in infrastructure, institutional arrangements for border and transit management systems, and the quality and operational performance of logistics services. Finally, the chapter explores the reasons why the current institutional arrangements have not fully addressed the main source of supply-chain inefficiencies and trade and transport bottlenecks.

The provision of transport infrastructure is a necessary, but not sufficient, condition for the movement of international trade and the efficient operation of the Euro-Asian supply chains. Obstacles and bottlenecks along transport routes in Central Asia occur because of technical barriers, the lack of policy, and problems with administrative interoperability and harmonization of legislation.

Physical barriers such as difficult terrain, poorly maintained roads and railways, or the absence of roads and railways can heavily impact trade and transportation flows. The current infrastructure seems to generally support the existing transportation flows, whereas the remaining missing links and the upgrade of existing links have received substantial attention as part of the national transport strategies of the respective governments (see chapter 4). In addition, quality modern specialized logistics facilities, such as inland container depots, in general are lacking to support the consolidation and distribution of goods and container transshipment between road and rail services.

## Fragmentation and Supply-Chain Bottlenecks

As shown in the examples in the previous chapters, supply chains linking Central Asian countries to each other and to the rest of the world are complex and sensitive to inefficiencies in one or the other areas listed above. Supply chains in

Central Asia are constrained by both geography and history. First, transit operates over long distances and generally involves many transport providers. Borders, especially with China, disrupt the supply chains. Furthermore, the legacy design of the supply chain from the breakup of the Soviet Union implies separate interventions such as the role of customs brokers and the obligation of going through a bonded warehouse. For these reasons, supply chains are especially fragmented and vulnerable. Reportedly, shippers and consignees have limited control on a supply chain, including when tracing goods in transit (a fact reflected in the Logistics Performance Index [LPI] scores).

Figure 6.1 illustrates the example of imports to Kazakhstan. Typically merchandise logistics includes three phases:

- International transit from the Russian Federation or China into Kazakhstan by truck or rail (rail wagons or containers), with intervention of transport companies, brokers, and forwarders.
- Clearance and warehousing in one of the main cities in Kazakhstan, with intervention of brokers and border agencies, and third-party logistics providers (3PLs) and
- Distribution logistics in Kazakhstan or Central Asia, with interventions of local transport companies.

**Figure 6.1 Supply-Chain Sequence in Kazakhstan**

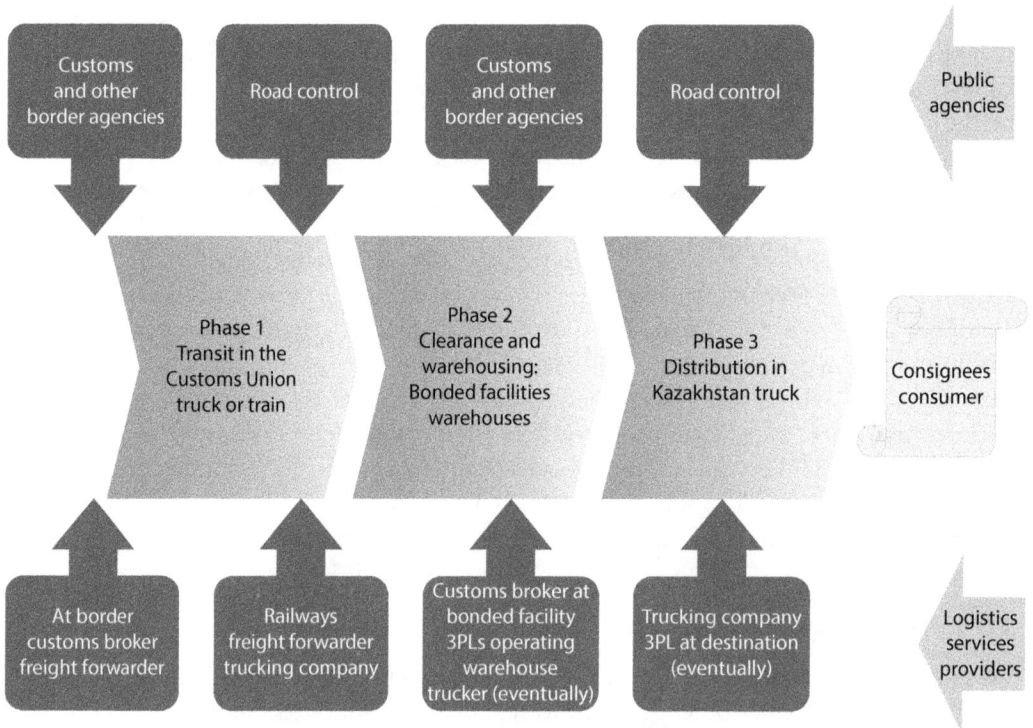

*Note:* 3PL = third-party logistics provider.

For other countries, the supply-chain sequence is the same (for instance, exports from China into the Kyrgyz Republic) or even more complicated, because it will include either reexport distribution from a logistics center in Kazakhstan, or transit through Kazakhstan with an additional border crossing.

Euro-Asian transit will essentially follow some of the same processes. For instance, the train, wagons, and containers are processed in the same way at the Customs Union (CU) borders (Dostyk or Khorgos at the Kazakhstan-China border) irrespective of whether the destination is a local inland terminal in Central Asia, Russia, or the European Union.

In the case of China, transport by truck is possible only from designated border areas, where Central Asian trucks load goods produced or stored in Xinjiang and import them to local Central Asian markets. Trains from China carry bulk commodities from Central Asia, and on the import side containers come from distant provinces in China.

As a result the full supply chain is very sensitive to inefficiencies in the processes, institutions, and service providers involved in the supply chain. The following reviews technical barriers, efficiency of services, railway transit, and trade facilitation for clearance of goods.

A field survey indeed shows that the main concerns of traders have to do with sources of unreliability (see box 6.1).

---

**Box 6.1  Voices of the Private Sector**

- We are using the Russian IT system ATEKO to track our trains because the Kazakh system is not very reliable.
- There is a lack of wagons/rolling stock, while the system of rail tariffs and recent changes are not very clear.
- Russian Railways imposes a shipping ban to Kazakhstan (and other countries, once every quarter) to limit their exposure to too many wagons outside their territory. We have to use trucks in this case to bring goods from Brest to Kazakhstan.
- The option of bringing goods from southeast China cannot be trusted either, as we experimented with 10+ wagons; the lead time would be about 40 days, but some wagons were held for 90 days, in part at the border.
- There is a lack of wagons during the harvest season so we cannot use rail to distribute our goods internally.
- Simplified procedures are not practical because they require a declaration within three hours of arrival, and arrival time is very unpredictable.
- Changes in the customs regulations are unpredictable.

*box continues next page*

The Eurasian Connection • http://dx.doi.org/10.1596/978-0-8213-9912-5

**Box 6.1  Voices of the Private Sector** *(continued)*

- Chinese goods come in transit through Estonia, being sourced from Hong Kong SAR, China. At this stage, the Chinese land route is not an option for us.
- Sometimes, the cost of shipping goods from the warehouse in Astana to the destination place within Astana can cost as much as shipping goods by truck from Almaty to Astana (1,200 km).

## Technical, Commercial, and Operational Constraints: Railways

As indicated earlier, the railways of Kazakhstan, the Kyrgyz Republic, Tajikistan, Turkmenistan, and Uzbekistan were until 1991 constituents of Soviet Railways, and the design standards implemented by each of these railways were, and still are, common to all. Consequently, for example, no technical obstacle exists to having rolling stock travel all the way from Lujaika (at the border between Finland and Russia) to Serakh in Turkmenistan. The obstacle, in this instance, seems more a question of policy among the railways concerned, because it is understood that some reluctance has been expressed by numerous Commonwealth of Independent States (CIS) railways to let their rolling stock run on the railways of other CIS republics. Whatever the reason for such reluctance, it must be recognized that container movements along railways will reach optimum operational efficiency only if rolling stock is allowed to cross borders.

The ongoing rail sector reforms in Kazakhstan and Russia are having some effect on the CIS-wide national pool of freight cars that smaller countries and railways relied upon. Once the fleets in Kazakhstan and Russia are considered private, for traffic originating in Kazakhstan and Russia, shippers needing wagons to load in the Kyrgyz Republic, Uzbekistan, and other CIS countries will be required to negotiate prices with private or unregulated wagon operators. Private rail transport prices within Kazakhstan and Russia are reportedly higher than the tariff prices (typically about 10 percent). However, prices will most likely be much higher in countries on the periphery of these much larger rail systems, because private wagon operators must pay for empty repositioning movements, and, as with any investor in an expansive asset, they value high wagon utilization (short wagon cycles).

For example, Kazakhstan Temir Jolu's (KTZ's) freight wagon fleet is aging and needs replacement. In 2009–10 nearly 67 percent of KTZ's freight fleet needed to be replaced in the next few years—about 45,000 wagons, expected to require an investment of more than $3 billion. Private investment in the wagon fleet has increased substantially in recent years. About 40,000 private wagons now operate in Kazakhstan, nearly 30,000 of which have been added in the last 10 years, representing a private investment of nearly $2 billion. However, most of this new private fleet is specialized or serves the largest shippers.

Technical barriers for rail transportation also relate to the operation of break-of-gauge stations or terminals in Kazakhstan, where the standard rail gauge

The Eurasian Connection • http://dx.doi.org/10.1596/978-0-8213-9912-5

(1,435 mm) meets the Russian gauge (1,525 mm). It appears that the transloading capacities from Russian to standard gauge are adequate, especially with the recent investment in Khorgos. Operational constraints appear to come not from the transloading itself but from the processing of transit containers, which is not related to the technical change in gauge.

The rail supply chain is a transit supply chain to or from a facility (container terminal or warehouse connected to the railways) to or from a third country such as China or Russia, or simply transit from China to Russia through Kazakhstan. The bottlenecks are similar in both cases, because the generic rail transit supply chain is fragmented for the same reasons whether or not the destination is Central Asia. Two bottlenecks in particular can be identified: (1) the continuity of transit across borders and (2) operational constraints with freight wagons and containers within Central Asian countries.

### Continuity of Transit: Tracking and Tracing

Facilitating information sharing on physical movement or documentation reduces fragmentation and improves reliability and also helps consignees trace and track their shipments. This is especially important when information about the goods being transported should follow trains across borders. The transloading operation is not constrained by the infrastructure. The main problem is the continuity of information between China and the CU.

The main source of supply-chain fragmentation seems to be the lack of traceability (ability to track) for forwarders on the wagons and boxes coming from China (unless a partner in China is doing the tracking and sharing the information) or at the border (because brokers are not passing information to forwarders or consignees, their role is limited to dealing only with customs and railways). Except in the case of a full train, such as is the case piloted by Hewlett Packard there has been no reliable information system so far. The container logistics is essentially push logistics from China. The eastbound traffic from Europe and Russia has a better tracking system, because European freight forwarders pass on the information about inbound containers, and the CIS railways' tracking system is reliable.

Many large companies have tried to import goods directly from China, mostly eastern China, but have given up on establishing permanent supply chains with that country. It seems that at the moment, imports from China are especially unreliable, and direct supply chains from the Chinese coastal production areas cannot be trusted either. One company experimented with 10 wagons from a supplier in the Guangdong region. The lead time would have been 40 days, but several wagons took almost 90 days. In part, the problem was that some wagons were lost at the border.

In reality, it seems to be very difficult to trace individual containers in transit before they are reloaded on a train in Dostyk or Khorgos by KTZ. The transit declaration is prepared by the customs broker in charge of the border bonded warehouse, based on the documentation received with the train from China. Freight forwarders assigned to the transaction are not directly informed by the broker or a Chinese counterpart.

The logical solution would be the intervention of international freight forwarders with the presence of all countries, with the international customers interested in consolidating container trains on the Europe-Asia land bridge. Their role would be to consolidate capacities on scheduled trains, track the trains with the railways in the country of transit, and pass the transit documentation across borders.

### Diseconomies of Scale and Terminal Inefficiencies

Moving a single freight wagon from a factory in Europe or China to a warehouse in Almaty or Astana involves a long series of logistics operations: cross-docking at the border, successive marshaling to a freight train bound for the destination cities, separation at the main station, and marshaling of a single unit to the warehouse within the urban railway network. The potential exists for significant delays. The terminal layout for distributing wagons and containers is a critical component of the chain, and the current layout is a source of major diseconomies of scale and logistics inefficiencies.

Trade needs not only the transport infrastructure but also specialized logistics facilities where nontransport activities are implemented efficiently: clearance, multimodal transfer, warehousing, and third-party logistics. The logical spatial hierarchy is as follows: a terminal such as a port serves one or several logistics centers hosting 3PL activities. Independent 3PLs' activities are "connected" to the terminal or to logistics centers. The hub of logistics activities is naturally the main economic and consumption centers. The (distribution) logistics of other parts of the countries are served by those hubs.

The problem is that the historical development of railways has encouraged substantial fragmentation of terminals in the region, where modern container logistics is based on high-volume scheduled train operations. Moving scheduled container trains without too many breakups depends on having relatively few destinations with high volume. The policies have not encouraged consolidation of freight and handling operations but rather the spreading out of terminal facilities within metropolitan areas and in the regions. Kazakhstan alone has about 30 container terminals, all small-scale operations.

About 10 terminals are in the Almaty area alone, the biggest handling about 30,000 twenty-foot equivalent units (TEUs) per year or about a train a day, which is a very low level of activity for the handling equipment on hand. Rather than having block trains, small volume implies having marshaling operations in the yard of the Almaty-I station, which results in additional delays and less predictable schedules (for one or two days). Each terminal has its own bonded warehouse and clearance, resulting in small-scale activities, a lesser degree of facilitation, and a low incentive for efficiency. In Almaty, containers need on average four more days to be cleared (it is not clear who or what is responsible for the delay).

From the perspective of transit logistics, concentrating the regional terminal operations in a few high-volume, high-efficiency "200,000 TEU+" dry ports would make possible much more effective connectivity of the regions both externally and internally.

## Technical, Commercial, and Operational Constraints: Road Transport

The condition of the road networks in the Central Asian republics is often poor. The main causes of poor road conditions are overloading of vehicles and lack of preventive maintenance because of funding constraints. This has led to a growing backlog of maintenance work. In the Kyrgyz Republic, for example, the road network is estimated to have lost about $1 billion in road assets because of the backlog in road maintenance and insufficient funding over the past two decades. Although the funds for improvement of regional roads will be sourced mainly from international financing institutions, financing road maintenance at the required level remains a challenge. As a result, much of the regional road network is now unsatisfactory and requires rehabilitation.

Improving the financing and management of roads to achieve sustainable development of the network requires government action. Road asset planning and management remains inefficient despite ongoing attempts by the governments of Kazakhstan, the Kyrgyz Republic, and Uzbekistan—with support from international financial institutions—to introduce road asset management systems to improve the planning, programming, and budgeting of road maintenance.

Additionally, several attempts have been made to transfer the responsibilities to improve, maintain, and operate roads to the private sector through contracting mechanisms. Capital repairs are predominantly executed by private construction companies, but only a few cases are seen in which routine road maintenance has been contracted to the private sector in the Central Asian region. Such exceptions include Tajikistan, where the operation and maintenance of the rehabilitated Dushanbe-Chanak road has been conceded to a private company under a public-private partnership scheme.

### Lack of Consistency in Standards and Enforcement

Although the lack of adequate maintenance policies and practices creates potentially serious bottlenecks for truck transportation, it is true that technical standards, norms, and parameters as well as their enforcement do so as well. It appears that Central Asian countries have developed idiosyncratic standards and enforcement practices in the absence of a common regional framework. They are not compatible from one country to another, meaning that one transit truck may be compliant with regulations on vehicle weight in one country but not the next. Although most Central Asian countries have signed the CIS Minsk Agreement (1999), which defines detailed maximum limits on road vehicle size and weight, the provisions of this agreement have yet to be incorporated into domestic legislation. For example, Kazakhstan has a 36-ton weight restriction, but the general agreement is based on 38 tons. Instead of trying to enforce a 36-ton weight limit, Kazakhstan could potentially save money and time by changing its transport law to a 38-ton weight limit.

The enforcement of technical standards, norms, and parameters is generally done in similar institutional arrangements in the countries of the Central Asia region, and plans exist to further develop and invest in national automated centralized systems of weighing stations, currently under consideration by most governments in the region. Transport control committees or agencies under the respective ministries responsible for transport generally carry out controls at specific posts in the close vicinity of customs checkpoints and usually installed in mobile vans or containers. Other restrictions such as the interruption of the movement of trucks based on specific temperatures (minus or plus) are reportedly enforced throughout the region and have important consequences for transportation movements. Tajikistan apparently prohibits daytime heavy truck traffic in the summertime when temperatures exceed 25 degrees (Celsius), whereas Kazakhstan reduced the authorized load by 50 percent in winter for certain areas.

Countries tend to restrict the flow of trucks from other countries. For instance, Uzbekistan reportedly prohibits entry of trucks from Tajikistan into its territory, and maintains a list of 800 products not allowed for transit. Tajik trucks can enter into the Kyrgyz Republic but cannot transit from China through the Kyrgyz Republic and have to take a higher seasonal route through the Pamir. The technical reason is that the agreements on trucking with China are purely bilateral and do not apply to trucks from a third country. The Transports Internationaux Routiers (TIR) trucks are not subject to those restrictions, because Central Asian countries abide with the TIR convention.

### Trucking (TIR)

The main services involved in supporting trade and logistics are trucking, freight forwarders, customs brokers, and third-party logistics (essentially warehousing in the local context). Only international trucking under TIR is following well-established international standards (see chapter 4). Most other logistics companies in the region do not offer very sophisticated services, operate under loosely defined regulations and professional standards, and are not integrated into the networks of global logistics companies.

The TIR operators have to work according to well-defined standards regarding the capacities of the companies and their vehicles (TIR convention). The national associations such as KAZATO in Almaty play an important role in supporting and organizing this industry. For example, in Kazakhstan, approximately 5,000 trucks participated in international traffic, with 268 companies registered as authorized TIR operators, in 2012. Kazakhstani road carriers, however, rarely collect goods in Europe from several countries during the same trip, because of the need for an additional bilateral entry permit. Although these permits seem to be in good supply, their usage is somewhat cumbersome. A license in such cases must be sent by courier service to the place of loading. This takes several days and adds to the costs.

However, registered international trucking is a very small share of trucking in the region. According to the Kazakhstan Statistics Agency, to date 414,000 trucks have been registered in Kazakhstan, but barely 1 percent of them are TIR operators. Not only cross-border trade between Central Asian countries but also trade with Chinese border areas is done out of the TIR.

## A Weak Regulatory Framework

Very surprisingly, requirements for domestic and regional non-TIR sectors are limited. Central Asia is one of the only world regions where entry into the trucking business is not regulated by considerations of professional qualifications. This means that any company or individual can sell commercial trucking services, provided he or she follows the general commercial code for companies or individual entrepreneurs, and the technical regulations put forward and enforced by the Transport Control Committee (working hours, safety standards, and axle-load limitations). The regulatory gap concerns these aspects:

- The distinction between transport of own-account (of one's own merchandise) and commercial freight transport services.
- The professional standards for trucking companies and their executives.

This gap in regulation is not conducive to the development of quality services, because of the potential of competition from unlicensed operators. It also promotes fragmentation of the industry. However, in the recent period of growth in demand, especially in Kazakhstan, organized specialized trucking companies could develop relatively well in the local market by offering specialized services (such as refrigeration), with limited competition from the traditional sector. This situation is relatively fragile: The history of other regions shows that, in the absence of proper regulation, the formal sector can be endangered by unfair competition when the demand is lower.

## Bottlenecks for Cross-Border Supply Chains and Trade Facilitation

Trade facilitation, in its original sense, is about making the processing of export, import, or transit clearance easier while preserving the social concerns at the origin of the procedure: fiscal revenue, health, consumer protection, road safety, and so on. Customs and border management remain a major agenda item in most countries in Central Asia and elsewhere. Most of the countries (Kazakhstan being more advanced) have yet to fully redevelop modern customs systems that can effectively reconcile the three objectives of raising fiscal revenue, facilitating trade, and protecting the consumer and the environment.

This convergence has taken a long time since the breakup of the Soviet Union, which unlike in transport infrastructure did not endow Kazakhstan with a trade facilitation soft infrastructure. It is also a critical element of World Trade Organization accession for the nonmember countries. There have been numerous improvements. For instance, since 2008 Kazakhstan has (1) reduced by a factor the level of physical inspection, (2) increased revenue per agent by 50 percent, and (3) reduced paperwork by incorporating standards and Sanitary and Phyto-Sanitary clearance under customs control.

The implementation of the provisions of the CU is also a "game changer" beyond Kazakhstan in at least two respects: it provides a modern customs code

The Eurasian Connection • http://dx.doi.org/10.1596/978-0-8213-9912-5

available in Russian, and it also suppressed the controls at the Russian borders, previously a problem area. Some major challenges still remain, however.

The first is the result of history. Some years ago the clearance system in Kazakhstan was quasi-privatized to customs brokers. It meant that clearance was largely delegated to brokers, which were given local monopolies on trade procedure. This situation created an incentive for collusion with customs staff and resulted in major cases of corruption, as uncovered recently in Khorgos. The current procedures have moved away from this practice, and responsibilities have been clarified. However, the present organization of supply chains and clearance is still dependent on a multitude of bonded "warehouses" of a private nature.

The second challenge is the dependence on international and national transit. Given their geographical location, landlocked status, and size, Central Asian countries are dependent not only on transit through third countries (including, for most trade, Kazakhstan), but also on imports that are preferably (about 93 percent) cleared after national transit at inland locations. Optimization of the transit regime is critical to reduce logistics costs and encourage activities such as transit through Kazakhstan. No regional transit regime is applicable for regional trade or transit from China. The CU regime applicable in Kazakhstan is better than previous systems. However, the current implementation of the CU transit regime is still much more complex and less friendly than the one in place for decades in the EU, which could be transposed to the region.

Another problem is the absence of communication between customs agencies across countries in the region, needed to trace goods in transit, facilitate transit by having the information from one country available to the next one, and limit the potential for fraud at the border. Governance within national borders is also a major constraint: Anecdotal evidence has been found of a high to very high level of informal payments on corridors. Informal payments are also associated with control and interventions, which all slow the speed of transit. Anecdotal evidence also suggests that informal payments can be very high. Truckers indicated that the suppression of the Russian-Kazakh border control saved $500 per round trip.

The duplication of controls is also a core issue in trade facilitation, which has until recently been a major problem in the region: in addition to customs clearance, the trader has to deal with health, phytosanitary, veterinary, and other agencies. In Kazakhstan, the Customs Control Committee (CCC) and the other agencies involved have made serious efforts to minimize paperwork and avoid duplication of control, processes referred to as integration of border management. Starting on January 27, 2010, Kazakhstan customs authorities at the road border crossings have been authorized to conduct transport control. The functions of veterinary, plant, and agriculture control are being transferred in 2013 under customs authority, at least for land borders. Other countries are rather less advanced in terms of border management. Typically three or four control agencies are found at international border posts, even when this is not justified by the volume of trade.

The areas of improvement have much to do with moving away from a pure and widespread control approach to a risk-based implementation of customs, where compliant traders receive expedited treatment. The concept of authorized trader does exist in the code. It could facilitate the management of regular supply chains, including for distribution of goods in Kazakhstan and the rest of Central Asia. In practice it is not very developed because the requirements are difficult to meet (for example, delays of submission and formalism), and experience is lacking that would help build a climate of trust. Effective implementation of such a regime, which is a complex undertaking, is a higher priority in large countries with a manufacturing base such as Kazakhstan and Uzbekistan.

In the smaller countries capacities are still weak with customs and other agencies. The problem is compounded in that the borders have been created after the road network and that many crossing routes do exist, in addition to the official crossing points. Price differentials tied to subsidies or different trade policies create incentives for rather large nonofficial flows. The authors observed in 2013, for instance, large reexports of Russian oil from the Kyrgyz Republic to Tajikistan. Eliminating such incentives for fraud will also help the modernization of the trade facilitation system.

The main areas where facilitation can be improved relatively easily in all countries include the suppression of paper-based declarations, the choice of a place of clearance, and better information about changes. Traders are also concerned with the lack of predictability and the uniformity of implementation across the country.

### Ancillary Services Freight Forwarding and Customs Brokerage

The role of freight forwarders is to organize international (or eventually domestic) logistics on behalf of shippers and consignees. This includes organizing transportation with railways and trucking companies as well as brokerage activities at the border. The role of customs brokers is more specific. They are accredited by customs authorities to fill out customs and transit declarations, and eventually perform other trade-related procedures, on behalf of a client.

The professions of freight forwarder and customs broker emerged with the breakup of the Soviet Union. The two activities have had a complex history over the years, especially for brokers, because of monopolistic tendencies and the lack of tools to properly regulate the sector. For historical reasons brokers are still very involved in customs procedures; in practice it is difficult to lodge a declaration without a broker.

The principles of regulation of customs brokers are based on licensing with financial guarantees and professional competence. The Eurasian Customs Union code applicable in Kazakhstan has import standards comparable to those of the EU. Brokers have to register with the CCC, and the requirements and penalties are more severe than they used to be.

As for trucking, in the cases of both forwarders and brokers, professional standards are loosely defined. Forwarders and brokers tend to have a narrower focus of activities than do similar companies in Europe, East Asia, or the Americas, where forwarders, for instance, typically offer brokerage services and the organization of transportation over several borders. Yet very few companies try to

The Eurasian Connection • http://dx.doi.org/10.1596/978-0-8213-9912-5

position themselves as integrated logistics providers and offer road transport operations by using their own trucks, freight forwarding by all modes of transport, as well as warehousing and brokerage services.

Many freight forwarders are practically agents for railway services. In Kazakhstan, where the sector is the largest, their contract with the railways takes the place of regulation and professional standards. Their role is quite limited in the organization of supply chains: they function essentially as commercial intermediaries between the railways and the shipper. Conversely, in Tajikistan, transport intermediaries are registered to market road services, but their role is much less than forwarding. In practice, shippers have to contract separately with the transport companies, the forwarders, and the brokers.

It does seem that logistics companies in Central Asia are poorly integrated into the global logistics network. Conversely, international companies have a discrete direct presence outside of the project logistics business, where they come with their international clients. The reasons for this disconnect may have to do with the current market structure and dependence on the railways and the lack of a well-defined and secure professional framework. Unfortunately this is a major hindrance to the development of efficient railway transit, which for the foreseeable future needs the intervention of international companies with a presence in three regions—Asia, Eurasia, and Europe.

There are exceptions. The lack of development of the sector also represents opportunities for operators and individuals with exposure to modern logistics outside the region to propose more comprehensive and reliable services. Few entrepreneurs have been able to develop modern logistics companies, for instance, with commodity exports such as cotton, or with project logistics.

Efforts to improve the regulations and the market structure face two major challenges. The first is the lack of incentives for change on the part of the local and regional operators; there is no international pressure. The second is that for Kazakhstan these regulations are now to be decided at the level of the Eurasian Customs Union, involving Russia. It is not just a matter of regional Central Asian cooperation.

## The Limitations of Cross-Border Cooperation in the Current Institutional Framework

The challenge of re-creating a trade and transportation scheme for countries in Central Asia and more generally the former Soviet Union (FSU) have been taken seriously for two decades by various institutions, with an intensification since the turn of the century. Unfortunately Central Asia does not escape the problem of the so-called "spaghetti bowl" where initiatives overlap with inconsistent country membership (figure 6.2). In Central Asia essentially three groups of initiatives are used to improve connectivity (Linn 2012): (1) corridor-based initiatives such as the Central Asia Regional Economic Cooperation (CAREC), (2) the Shanghai Cooperation Organization (SCO) supported by China, and (3) the Eurasian Customs Union, led by Russia.

**Figure 6.2  The "Spaghetti Bowl" of Regional Organizations in Central Asia**

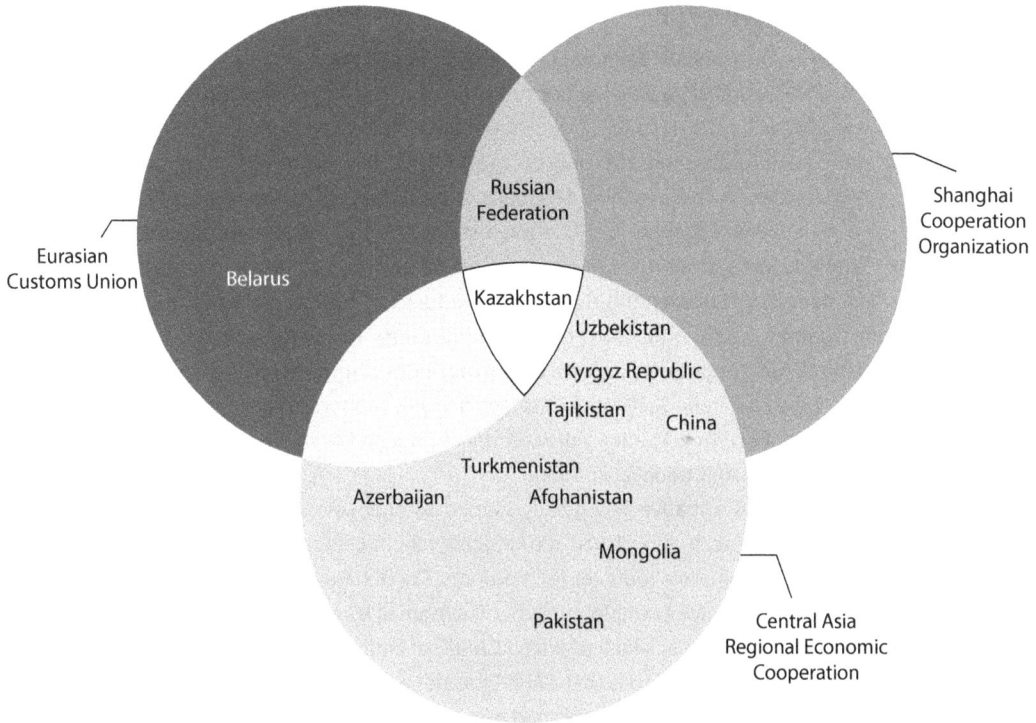

*Note:* AFG = Afghanistan; AZE = Azerbaijan; BLR = Belarus; CAREC = Central Asia Regional Economic Cooperation; CHN = China; KAZ = Kazakhstan; KGZ = Kyrgyz Republic; MNG = Mongolia; PAK = Pakistan; RUS = Russian Federation; SCO = Shanghai Cooperation Organization; TJK = Tajikistan; TKM = Turkmenistan; UZB = Uzbekistan.

Until the Eurasian initiative entered into its implementation phase beginning in 2011, the focus in Central Asia has been on initiatives concerning the development of specific routes (box 6.2), including road and rail corridors. These initiatives have been effective, because they have created a more or less institutionalized framework governed by a secretariat, such as CAREC, as a sponsoring organization. However, the issue of deeper integration between the countries to address the needs of cross-border or transit logistics has failed to be resolved under such a framework because of the organization's focus and its lack of mandate on operational, commercial, governance, and regulatory issues. Although the focus on corridors in the regions has contributed to advocating the need for further integration, the role of corridor initiatives so far has been positive in promoting the facilitation agenda with policy makers or stakeholders, notably due to the development of indicators. These initiatives have also contributed to facilitation of cross-border dialogue on the ground to expedite clearance of cross-border and transit trade, notably in Central Asia. Finally, corridor initiatives have been very helpful in coordinating the international agencies providing support to infrastructure and reforms.

## Box 6.2  Main Corridor Initiatives in the Central Asia Region

### CAREC—Central Asia Regional Economic Cooperation

The CAREC is initially a development initiative from the Asian Development Bank (ADB), which was initiated in 2001. CAREC brings together 10 member countries and international organizations including the ADB and the World Bank. Beyond the five Central Asian republics, Afghanistan, Azerbaijan, China, Mongolia, and Pakistan are members of CAREC.

As its name suggests, CAREC's interests go beyond the development of transport corridors to include energy connectivity and other forms of economic cooperation among its members. However, the quasi-exclusive focus of CAREC has been trade and transport facilitation on six priority corridors linking China to Russia and the Caucasus through Central Asia (http://www.carecprogram.org/index.php?page=carec-corridors). The CAREC Transport and Trade Facilitation Strategy in 2007 supported these efforts by introducing a program of action featuring mutual cooperation and key investments in regional transport infrastructure and trade facilitation.

The CAREC initiative has greatly helped to channel technical assistance and funding for the corridors. It also played the greatest role in creating awareness and provided performance monitoring tools on the corridors. The initiative had much less impact on core national reforms (for example, customs). There are at least two unfavorable factors. The first is the absence of Russia, which deprived CAREC of critical leverage on the main logistics flows in the region. The second is that CAREC has not acquired the profile of a regional economic commission. CAREC is not established by a treaty under binding principles that would shape the reforms in the member countries. Furthermore, CAREC is a forum of experts within a development program. Little direct participation is found by political leaders who should be the promoters of integration at a higher level.

### Other Corridor Initiatives

### TRACECA

The earliest effort to develop trade corridors in the region was started in 1993 by the European Union with its Transport Corridor Europe-Caucasus-Asia (TRACECA) initiative. The TRACECA corridor touches the southern part of the region, with branches along the following countries: Armenia, Azerbaijan, Bulgaria, Georgia, the Islamic Republic of Iran, Kazakhstan, the Kyrgyz Republic, Moldova, Romania, Tajikistan, Turkey, Ukraine, and Uzbekistan.

### UNESCAP

One of the other pioneering agencies to develop the modern concept of the Asian trade corridors was the UN Economic and Social Commission for Asia and the Pacific (UNESCAP). Beginning in the late 1950s it developed the concept of an Asian Highway Network (141,000 km and 32 countries) and a Trans-Asian Railway Network. It includes a northern corridor connecting the rail networks of China, Kazakhstan, Mongolia, Russia, and the Korean Peninsula. UNESCAP has advocated the feasibility and the establishment of regular rail services from China to Europe through Russia and Kazakhstan.

*box continues next page*

**Box 6.2  Main Corridor Initiatives in the Central Asia Region** *(continued)*

**New Eurasian Land Transport Initiative (IRU 2011)**

A more recent initiative has been made by the International Road Transport Union under the name New Eurasian Land Transport Initiative Project. Its aim is to better understand regular road freight shipments between Europe and China and to assist in achieving the transit potential of nations in Central Asia and the Caucasus.

---

## *Limits to the Effectiveness of the Corridor Approach*

First and foremost, the corridor initiative is not a substitute for deeper integration within a region (although it may be a first step in the right direction) that can effectively address harmonization and integration of border control and provide an open and harmonized framework for the movement of vehicles, especially trucks. The TIR transit regime to which the regional countries are parties (with the exception of China) provides the default solution for long-distance trade by road. The TIR does not posit a regional harmonized framework for trade, customs, and transportation, but rather assumes chained trucking activities across borders with a common customs guarantee managed by the International Road Transport Union (IRU). The FSU corridor initiatives are essentially additional to the TIR.

There have been many different specifications of land transport corridors through Central Asia, and these have resulted in more than 60 corridors being considered by the various agencies involved. The mere proliferation of and de facto competition between initiatives, often by international agencies on different continents or belonging to different groupings, present a clear limitation.

In Central Asia especially, the corridor concept so far has not solved fundamental issues concerning institutional capacity and private sector competence. Most of the binding constraints are not route specific; they are structural issues found to various degrees in all countries but are largely national. They have to be addressed at the national level, eventually within a regional integration framework with a strong customs and transport component, such as the Eurasian Customs Union and/or the SCO (see boxes 6.3 and 6.4).

Political issues between countries are not only an obvious obstacle to regional integration, but they impact trade directly through closed borders or strong limitations. Furthermore, the corridor initiatives are primarily technical assistance projects and expert forums where high-level policy makers do not participate. Hence, in many decisions that matter, many experts have been taken out of the corridor dialogue.

Finally, the focus of interventions in trade and transport facilitation has been on more road corridors, leaving out railway freight, which is constrained by some of the same issues such as capacity of the control agencies such as customs. However, the cross-border integration of railway operations between national companies and the improvement of their operational performance have received much less attention than road corridors, even though they are critical to the regional supply chains.

The Eurasian Connection  •  http://dx.doi.org/10.1596/978-0-8213-9912-5

## Box 6.3  Trade and Transport Facilitation in the Eurasian Customs Union

Following the creation of the Customs Union (CU) between Kazakhstan, Belarus, and Russia and the Common Economic Space, member countries are still in the process of defining their exclusive, shared, and national powers within CU.

Being the successor to the abolished Customs Union Commission (CUC), the Eurasian Economic Commission (EEC), created on November 18, 2011, has as its main objective to provide a favorable environment for the functioning and development of the CU and the Common Economic Space and to develop proposals for further integration. In addition to customs and tariff regulations, customs administration, and technical regulations previously performed by the CUC, the EEC is charged with the establishment of trade regimes with third countries; coordination of agreed monetary, macroeconomic, energy, and competition policies; regulation of natural monopolies; government subsidies to industry and agriculture; and harmonization of public procurement legislation in the fields of transport, migration, and regulation of financial markets.

The EEC has competence in (among other areas) customs, freight transport, and logistics. Given the cross-border nature of logistics, in the medium term it should be expected that most of the logistics-related regulations should have an EEC source, as in the European Union.

Indeed, in the context of supply chain and logistics, decisions taken at the CU level and the corresponding legal framework appear to be fully developed. They are being adopted by the Kazakhstani authorities, especially in the areas of customs clearance (adherence to a common customs code) and the railways. These regulations are discussed further in chapter 5. Unlike these regulations, the legal framework for the trucking industry or logistics services has not been fully developed; this is reflected in the existing gaps in national legislation on the operation of trucks.

## Box 6.4  The Shanghai Cooperation Organization

The Shanghai Cooperation Organization (SCO) was created in 2001 and includes China, Kazakhstan, the Kyrgyz Republic, Russia, Tajikistan, and Uzbekistan.

The SCO is a political, security, and economic organization with its secretariat based in Beijing. The creation of the SCO reflects the growing role that China plays in Central Asia. China lends to infrastructure projects such as roads and railroads in the Central Asian region (Dzyubenko 2012). China is investing in oil and gas and industrial capacities, notably in Kazakhstan and Turkmenistan.

The SCO has been an effective forum for high-level discussions between China and the Central Asian countries and Russia. However this arrangement has not been given the prerogative of an actual economic commission. SCO does not include to date an implementation arm that would look at, for instance, trade, transport, and economic integration bottlenecks and design common solutions.

*Source:* Linn 2012.

# References

Dzyubenko, Olga. 2012. "China to Expand C. Asian Presence with $10 bln in Loans." *Reuters*. December 5. http://www.reuters.com/article/2012/12/05/china-centralasia -idUSL5E8N59DS20121205.

Linn, Johannes. 2012. "Central Asian Regional Integration and Cooperation: Reality or Mirage?" In *Eurasian Integration Yearbook 2012*, 96–117. Almaty: Eurasian Development Bank.

IRU (International Road Transport Union). 2011. *An Analysis of Goods Flow in Central Asia and Border Regions of China, Executive Summary*. Moscow. http://www.iru-nelti .org/index/en_publications.

CHAPTER 7

# Improving the Eurasian Connection

Not surprisingly, connecting Central Asian countries along the modern Silk Route to markets is a very daunting task. The countries in the region, although very heterogeneous economically and diverse geographically, are facing similar constraints. Institutions, business logistics, and the post-Soviet fragmentation are impacting supply-chain efficiency, both regionally for imports and exports and when connecting to Europe and Asia. The way forward should combine persistence in national reforms (customs, trade facilitation, and transportation) with more openness to private sector participation in key operations (notably, railways).

Reducing the fragmentation of supply chains implies a renewed push for cross-border integration in such areas as infrastructure standards, trade facilitation, and services regulation. The scope of cross-border cooperation goes beyond the existing corridor initiatives and will benefit from the spillover of measures taken or to be taken at the level of the Eurasian Customs Union (customs code and transport regulations), the implementation of which should start with Kazakhstan.

## Challenges and Opportunities in Advancing the Connectivity Agenda

The commodity-oriented structure of the economies in Central Asia and their landlocked geographic location, with the long distance to European and East Asian partners, are not the only causes of the slow pace of reforms to improve services and processes for trade supply chains. Nor is the regional political economy, where often a lack of cooperation between countries has slowed trade and transportation initiatives.

Trade supply chains are only as strong as their weakest link; hence progress made in one area such as infrastructure may not compensate for a lack of progress or slower progress in other areas such as the quality of logistics services, trade facilitation, and oftentimes a lack of cooperation.

The main sources of trade costs and supply-chain inefficiencies have very much to do with the fragmentation of logistics across and within borders.

The reliance on long transit routes for all types of trade is one source of complexity: in the case of Uzbekistan, for example, goods have to flow in transit through the Russian Federation, China, and Kazakhstan to reach Uzbekistan. Another source of complexity and fragmentation is a result of historical factors and comes from the organization of trade set in place after the collapse of the Soviet Union.

Until very recently, the design of supply chains has been developed on a country-by-country basis, with a strong focus on control rather than trade facilitation. As a result, the role of national logistics intermediaries such as customs brokers has been elevated, which has resulted in additional fragmentation as opposed to the achievement of greater cross-border integration.

Governments in Central Asia are aware of the importance of the agenda, but so far there have been few consistent actions, both within countries as well as between them. Separation of administrative responsibilities does not help tackle cross-cutting topics such as logistics. It means that the incentives of independent agencies are not aligned with the collective action of improving supply chains. For instance, ministries of transportation are incentivized to build infrastructure rather than to improve the quality of services or to open national markets to foreign providers. To address some of these coordination issues, the government of Kazakhstan set up an interagency committee on logistics in 2012.

One major regional weakness in designing consistent connectivity strategies is the lack of a strong, organized base of export-oriented manufacturers. The demand for reform and pressure on governments has therefore not been fueled by a public-private debate on national logistics efficiency in the way it has been in Central Asian countries (see box 7.1). In policy making, the private sector is typically associated with quasi-administrative business association representatives of local truckers, forwarders, and/or customs brokers and representatives. The discussion may be biased toward addressing the needs of mass transportation of bulk items, which usually do not require modern logistics, in contrast to time-sensitive commodities. Unlike in Europe or Asia, very little voice is given to the users of logistics who actually suffer from the supply-chain inefficiencies, such as retail companies or exporters of manufactured and time-sensitive goods.

---

**Box 7.1  Public-Private Logistics Strategies**

Most Organisation for Economic Co-operation and Development economies have private or public-private forums on logistics, such as the Council of Supply Chain Management (the United States), ASLOG (France), and Dinalog (the Netherlands). Such platforms would bring together providers and users of logistics as well as the public sector. In Central Asia, they would create the enabling environment to build strategic partnerships, which could bring innovations and bridge the gaps between different logistics services.

---

*box continues next page*

**Box 7.1  Public-Private Logistics Strategies** *(continued)*

Dinalog (www.dinalog.nl) is a particularly relevant example of public-private partnership to promote and make logistics more efficient in a country that serves as a major hub and transit gateway to Europe. Dinalog, the Dutch Institute for Advanced Logistics, was founded in 2009 to provide the best means to achieve this and to maintain a leading position in logistics and supply-chain management. Dinalog is fully embraced by the business world, trade organizations, main ports, authorities, and knowledge institutions. Dinalog has an institute and a campus to foster "open innovation," bridge the gaps between services, and encourage strategic cooperation in which air, railway, road, and river transport services work together as one. Dinalog is, therefore, devoted to developing scientific knowledge for advanced logistics with worldwide acknowledgment in both the academic and business communities. The aim is to create an environment that attracts world-class international researchers and where innovative companies are willing to base their key professionals to work on improving supply-chain and logistics management. Dinalog is engaged in global partnerships with major institutions such as the World Bank.

---

Furthermore, the situation is exacerbated by a lack of skills and a limited culture of supply-chain management among private and public sector managers. Limited presence of international logistics companies implies limited exposure to international best practices in the field of supply-chain management. The Central Asian region is one of the most isolated from international logistics knowledge. As proposed below, greater involvement of global logistics operators aiming to facilitate long-distance transit would lead to greater spillovers in the region.

## Implementation Dynamics and Drivers for Change

Strong commonalities are found between the requirements and remedies for improving trade and transport connectivity at all three levels of trade and transit: regional trade, international connectivity, and Euro-Asian transit through Central Asia. The focus is on making logistics efficient, both domestically and regionally.

The hub-and-spokes nature of the trade and transport connectivity should be recognized as well. Larger countries, including Kazakhstan and Russia, play a particularly important role for both intraregional and transcontinental transit trade given their strategic location (most transit logistics happens in their territory) and market dominance in the regional service industry.

The implementation of the Customs Union (CU) and the increased presence of China are likely to encourage significant changes, both in the institutions that facilitate trade and in the way the private sector operates and establishes trade and transport connections in the region. The Eurasian Customs Union has had some positive impact, at least on the northern routes of the former Soviet Union (FSU). Since customs control between borders of the Union members has been phased out, the CU has a direct facilitation impact. Reportedly, it also helped simplify trade with the non-Union countries because the CU member countries share a single transit system for goods flowing through their territory.

The CU also facilitates the integration of transport services (such as railways) and improves the possibilities for trucks to operate across borders.

Whether the CU should include other Central Asian countries besides Kazakhstan is beyond the scope of this work, because in addition to logistics other dimensions to this question exist (fiscal, trade policy, and so forth). As demonstrated by the case of Kazakhstan, a CU is a major simplification that helps connect both within the Union and internationally. It dramatically reduces the sources of fragmentation and provides a framework to solve some of the core issues, such as transit and regulation of services. As the EU trade and transport procedures have expanded to the nonmember countries close to the EU, and associated to it (for example, the Balkans, Morocco, Turkey), the common "acquis" from the Eurasian Customs Union should influence the change in rules and regulations in Central Asia regardless of whether the countries join the CU. Given the trade pattern and the integration of logistics operators in the FSU, idiosyncratic measures will have a cost.

The strong interest of the government of China to develop and facilitate overland trade with the region is tied to the country's strategy to further develop its western provinces (see box 7.2). Major rail infrastructure is being completed to increase the capacity toward Kazakhstan and the Kyrgyz Republic. Special zones are being created at borders such as Khorgos (Xinjiang Province in China and Kazakhstan). This policy already shows a gradual reorientation of trade of the eastern FSU countries (Kazakhstan and the Kyrgyz Republic) toward China.

Given recent history, two existing organizations are likely to play a complementary role in the implementation and monitoring of connectivity enhancement packages. The first is obviously Central Asia Regional Economic Cooperation (CAREC), including more generally the group of international agencies such as the World Bank and the Asian Development Bank (ADB). These should continue to play a major role in facilitating provision of financing or technical assistance for missing links of regional importance. The production of regular monitoring indicators by CAREC is equally very important to the program.

However, supply-chain-related measures and reforms are likely to be driven by the convergence toward the "acquis" of the CU, whether the countries are formally part of the CU or not. Idiosyncratic development country by country would not be sustainable, as is currently the case. Much of the design and implementation of regulatory changes and implementation should involve expertise from the CU.

---

**Box 7.2  Policies to Develop Western China**

The initiatives by the government of China gave an additional incentive to the increase in Chinese freight transit through Kazakhstan to the European Union. The Chinese government is making considerable efforts to develop the Xingjian-Uighur Autonomous Region adjacent to Kazakhstan. The integrated Chinese great leap transport strategy and the

*box continues next page*

**Box 7.2  Policies to Develop Western China** *(continued)*

Go West Program for accelerated development of China's western provinces are designed to bridge the gap between the economically advanced coastal areas of China and the less advanced western regions of the country. To achieve this objective, the government is going to accelerate the development of its infrastructure, including the transport infrastructure; invest in new production facilities; create incentives to attract foreign capital; develop the education system; and attract professional labor to this promising region. Implementation of these programs will create preconditions for the establishment of additional export-oriented production facilities and conditions for an increase in cargo traffic in the immediate proximity of the Republic of Korea. Having created favorable conditions for transit and removed existing physical and nonphysical barriers, Korea can play a role in crossing the land bridge between the East and the West and opening the way for goods from western China to reach Europe.

The Chinese industrial park on the Chinese side of Khorgos covers 9.73 square km of land. It already has more than 30 production companies on site. The Chinese Khorgos has about 10 different wholesale markets, with more than 500,000 square meters of warehouses for storage of merchandise. In 2011 the volume of trade through the Border Crossing Post exceeded $7 billion, and more than 16,000 trucks crossed the border, almost all of this resulting from Chinese exports. In China, Khorgos is positioned as the western Shenzhen, which is expected to develop quickly because of trade with its western partners and to grow into a city with around 200,000 residents. Ansher Investment's research shows that financing for new trade and logistics projects along the new Silk Route will not be a problem, given the high interest in this region among more than 2,000 private equity and venture capital investment funds in China.

## Specific Measures to Improve Connectivity

It is proposed to structure the agenda along four broad measures that have to be implemented either nationally or across countries. Unlike the current corridor approach, they are not corridor specific. These measures are expected to lead to an increase in the handling capacity of land transport routes and their reliability, as well as a subsequent reduction in transportation costs and lead times.

### 1. Improving the Quality of Transportation Links and Cross-Border Connectivity

Although some technical characteristics of the road and rail infrastructure on specific road sections and railway links need to be tackled (upgrading to support higher axle loads, electrification, and so forth), these issues can be addressed with simple financing and international good practice.

Most of the proposed transportation links are currently under rehabilitation and/or are expected to be addressed in the near future along the north-south and east-west axes, such as the remaining sections of the Bishkek-Osh-Isfana road (the Kyrgyz Republic), the Western Europe–Western China transit corridor (Kazakhstan), the road links along the A380 highway (Uzbekistan), sections along the Dushanbe-Karamick road corridor, and others. On the railway side, several rail links are currently being upgraded and electrified, foremost the rail line between Tashkent and Termez (Uzbekistan), the line connecting Khorgos and Almaty (Kazakhstan), and the north-south rail link in Turkmenistan toward Serakh. Most of those links will substantially contribute to the further development of the existing transportation networks of the respective countries, with the purpose of increasing transportation movements for domestic economic activities and regional trade.

Programs and support for the planning and budgeting of road maintenance of the recently rehabilitated and to some extent upgraded assets will have to be increased to ensure proper maintenance of the new assets. Technical assistance is currently ongoing in most countries (especially Kazakhstan, the Kyrgyz Republic, and Uzbekistan) on the introduction of road asset management systems that should introduce efficient programming, planning, and budgeting of maintenance. Sufficient financing for maintenance has to be allocated by the respective governments.

At the same time, most governments in the region are currently pursuing the development of new road and rail links to further develop and integrate their transportation networks at the national and regional level. Those investments, for example, include the Zhezkazgan-Beineu rail link (Kazakhstan), the Angren-Pap rail link (Uzbekistan), the north-south and east-west links (the Kyrgyz Republic), and the Tajikistan-Afghanistan-Turkmenistan rail link. Economic evaluation should determine the attractiveness of and rationale for those new links, in particular their strategic importance for the development of an integrated rail and road network at the regional level with facilitation of cross-border connectivity.

*Objectives:* These are (1) improving the quality of transport links and (2) developing an integrated road and rail network that not only serves national interests but supports further integration of the transportation network at the regional (cross-border) level.

*Components:* Significant progress has been achieved in raising the quality of transportation links in the region, which has had substantial impacts on the movement of freight and goods. However, new projects need to assess the cost-effectiveness of the investments and analyze their specific impact on improving connectivity within the region and the outside.

1.1. *Improve existing road and railway links* along the east-west and north-south axes to efficiently address transportation demand and present the status of ongoing rehabilitation/upgrade at regional forums such as CAREC.

1.2. *Focus on adequate maintenance policies and financing:* This implies detailed analysis of future maintenance needs and requirements at the national level, an introduction of planning tools, and a firm commitment by the governments to adequate financing. The introduction of private companies to operate and maintain assets could be considered where the current pilots are shown to be successful.

1.3. *Re-create cross-border road and rail links of regional importance:* With the breakup of the Soviet Union, the road and rail networks disintegrated, requiring countries to focus on improving internal communications within each new state rather than strengthening the regional network. Similarly, the development of transit potential involves elements of competition because each country has stated its preference for as much transit as possible to go through its territory. Although diversification of transport routes is a natural process in the search for means to reduce transport costs, it has resulted in a nonconducive environment that has often neglected road and rail links of regional importance. The connections in the Ferghana Valley are an example of this.

## 2. Moving Containers Efficiently: Europe and East Asia Rail Freight

Most rail transit going through Kazakhstan's borders with China or Russia terminates inland in Kazakhstan or serves other Central Asian countries. The share of China-Russia-Europe transit traffic is still a very small part of the total freight bound for the region. Both Central Asian and Europe-Asia logistics face problems of efficiency and fragmentation of the transit supply chain. One issue is the lack of continuity of rail transit between China and the CU, which contributes to the inability to trace transported freight and containers from their origin to the transloading facility at the border.

Another problem is the apparent lack of reliable schedules for container and freight wagons, which is an operational problem compounded by the fragmentation of small-scale terminal facilities. It makes it difficult to have reliable and scheduled services both for regional and Eurasian transit.

The successful experiment with block trains through Kazakhstan was made possible because numerous multinational companies organized the transit of goods in cooperation with the railway operators and customs authorities in each country of transit (see Model 1 in box 3.3). At the moment, no regular scheduled service is available that would allow consolidating containers from various shippers on the same train. This next step (moving to Model 2 in box 3.3) implies establishing a partnership between global forwarders in China, the Commonwealth of Independent States (CIS), and Europe that would allow (1) handling and consolidating the freight from several clients on the same block train, organizing transit in cooperation with the railway operators and customs and (2) being able to track and trace across borders.

*Objectives:* (1) The creation of reliable scheduled container services and (2) reorganization of the terminal system to generate the economies of scale needed for the scheduled container service to operate directly from terminal to terminal, without reassembling the trains.

*Components:* Much remains to be achieved, primarily in Kazakhstan, which is pivotal for both Euro-Asian transit and transit to the Central Asian countries.

2.1. *Establish or reinforce alliances with international freight forwarders and railways* in China and Russia to be able to experiment with consolidated services organized by international freight forwarders. This would also include the expansion of scheduled container block trains to selected priority terminals in Central Asian countries other than Kazakhstan (for example, Uzbekistan).

2.2. *Consolidate scheduled trains on fewer terminals:* This implies a discussion with Kazakhstan Temir Jolu (KTZ) and private terminal owners to determine the optimal destination of block trains in Kazakhstan and Central Asian destination countries. It may imply the planning of a larger terminal (with a capacity of 100,000 twenty-foot equivalent units or more).

2.3. *Establish a continuous "track and trace" system for transit merchandise:* This is mostly the responsibility of international freight forwarders. A better protocol on exchange of information should be set up to facilitate transit, notably at the CU border, between operators and trading companies, customs (notably the Customs Control Committee [CCC] in Kazakhstan), and international freight forwarders.

### 3. Enhancing the Role of the Private Sector in the Provision of Logistics Services

The logistics industry in Central Asia is not very well developed or integrated with the global logistics industry. Freight forwarders, third-party logistics services and customs brokers are essentially local companies that have no international linkages and provide a limited range of services. Forwarders typically operate under contracts with the railways, for which they act like agents: they have no exclusive connections with international logistics companies. This poor state of the logistics industry serves as a major constraint to developing the role of Central Asia as a land bridge, as well as a major source of fragmentation of supply chains going through China, Kazakhstan, and Russia. It is a barrier to partnerships with international companies that can help connect the Silk Route countries.

Domestic trucking has no regulation of entry or distinction between commercial trucking and own-account activities. Such a distinction exists in most countries and serves as a base for better sector competition, as well as a precondition for sound sector development. In Central Asia, it is only the small segment of international Transports Internationaux Routiers (TIR) trucking that has very well defined industry standards due to the need for compliance with the TIR system.

*Objective:* The objective is to align professional standards and regulation of entry with international practices to improve quality of service and facilitate the emergence of players of regional importance, who can be a part of international logistics networks.

In practice such changes have to be implemented identically in all countries to avoid the cost of idiosyncratic regulations as they exist now. These measures should be driven by an "acquis" from the improvement of the regulatory framework for logistics services within the Eurasian Customs Union countries, including Kazakhstan. Implementation in the other countries may follow at a different pace depending on their participation in the CU and capacity for reform.

*Components:* The main regulatory areas include the following:

3.1. *Develop professional standards for truckers* consistent with international standards, and separate commercial activities from own-account transportation. This could be supported through technical assistance to facilitate the conversion of existing operators.

3.2. *Define the role of freight forwarders* according to international standards and not just as commercial agents to the railway companies (for example, Kazakhstan). The status of transport brokers that are developed in certain countries (for example, Tajikistan) should be aligned with that of the freight forwarders.

3.3. *Align the regulation of customs brokers* with international best practices.

## 4. Expanding Trade and Transit Facilitation Initiatives

At the moment, the trade facilitation framework is still in transition, with compliance with international best practices and encouragement of compliant private operators still underdeveloped. As a result, the organization of customs clearance processes has only partially moved away from the legacy systems characterized by bonded warehouses, paper documentation, and de facto quasi-indispensable intervention of customs brokers.

Another feature is the role of transit, because most import goods for consumption are not cleared at the border but almost entirely at inland destinations, near the economic centers. The CU transit regime is applied in a way that seems to deviate from international practices (it is more complex with less freedom for compliant transit operators). Kazakhstan plays a pivotal role in transit.

*Objective:* The objective is to make the clearance and transit processes friendlier to traders, while securing national fiscal interests. This should happen through a transition to a compliance-based system of customs clearance, with use of authorized-trader schemes or the equivalent. Under such a system, economic operators with a positive track record of compliance that meet accounting and financial standards (for example, bonds and guarantees) would be entitled to expedited treatment.

*Components:* The following areas should be targeted as priorities with eventually differentiated needs:

4.1. *Institute paperless customs declaration and enhance customs capacity*, allowing at least regular traders to submit their customs declarations online, without the intervention of customs brokers. This should be accompanied by support in the area of risk management.

4.2. *Facilitate the development of authorized economic operators/traders:* It might be difficult to implement the authorized-trader regime on a regional basis, but it should be encouraged on a country basis, at least in the large economies. Existing requirements may be streamlined without creating fiscal risk or deviating from international best practices (for instance, ownership of facilities, submission deadlines, and auditing procedures). Priority should be given to countries with larger manufacturing or wholesale operators (such as Kazakhstan and Uzbekistan).

4.3. *Improve the implementation of the CU transit regime in Kazakhstan and Russia,* which in practice means proposing solutions to align the internal CU transit implementation mechanism with that of the European Union common transit procedure. This component does not require special discussions with the private sector but rather implies consultations with the experts on the European Union common transit procedure.

4.4. *Facilitate transit and cross-border trade through interconnection of the transit information systems in the regional countries:* The countries in the region have computerized trade systems. Protocols for the exchange of information would help facilitate transit and manage cross-border trade. For instance, for the importing country, the ability to access information on exporters from the neighboring country would facilitate the implementation of rules of origin and the control of fraud and smuggling. It is recommended to start with a pilot pair of countries where information technology systems are developed, such as Kazakhstan and the Kyrgyz Republic. This action would be required for accession to the CU.

4.5. *Phase out existing obstacles to transit by trucks,* including (1) restrictive lists of products allowed for transit and (2) restriction of passage of non-TIR trucks from a country in the region. This would include the consolidation of existing bilateral agreements on permits with China, so that trucks from any origin within Central Asia can pick up deliveries at the border and transit through third countries.

## Summarizing the Impact

**Table 7.1  How Measures in the Plan of Action Will Impact Various Dimensions of Supply-Chain Performance According to the Six Logistics Performance Index Categories**

| Dimensions in logistics performance | Quality of trade and transport-related infrastructure | Efficiency of customs (border) clearance process | Competence and quality of logistics services | Ease of arranging competitively priced international shipments | Ability to track and trace consignments | Timeliness |
|---|---|---|---|---|---|---|
| Infrastructure assets | most impact | some impact | limited impact | no impact | limited impact | some impact |
| Moving containers | some impact | some impact | significant impact | significant impact | most impact | most impact |
| Regulation of logistics services | no impact | limited impact | most impact | significant impact | some impact | significant impact |
| Trade and transit facilitation | no impact | most impact | some impact | significant impact | significant impact | significant impact |

*Note:* ◯ = no impact, ◖= limited impact, ◐ = some impact, ◔ = significant impact, ● = most impact.

# Overview on Initiatives for Technical and Financial Coordination and Development of Land Routes through Central Asia

The initiatives by Central Asia Regional Economic Cooperation (CAREC), Transport Corridor Europe-Caucasus-Asia (TRACECA), and the New Eurasian Land Transport Initiative (NELTI), and the dedicated initiatives within the United Nations Economic Commission for Europe (UNECE) created a framework of strategies for technical and financial coordination and development of land corridors, transport infrastructure, and trade. All these initiatives acknowledge the importance that transport and trade play in the promotion of economic growth and socioeconomic development. However, differences are seen in the approaches related to the regions and transport modes they cover. The NELTI initiative concentrates on road development, whereas those of CAREC, TRACECA, and UNECE cover both rail and road transport. CAREC's and TRACECA's initiatives include the transport of passengers, whereas NELTI's encompasses only the delivery of goods.

The CAREC program is a partnership between Afghanistan, Azerbaijan, China, Kazakhstan, the Kyrgyz Republic, Mongolia, Pakistan, Tajikistan, Turkmenistan, and Uzbekistan and involves six multilateral institutions: the Asian Development Bank, the European Bank for Reconstruction and Development, the International Monetary Fund, the Islamic Development Bank, the United Nations Development Programme, and the World Bank. Launched in 1997, it aims to promote regional cooperation in transport, trade facilitation, trade policy, and energy.

The NELTI was established in 2008 under the organization of the International Road Transport Union (IRU). Implemented in three phases, the NELTI road network has shown that the existing road infrastructure is sufficient to undertake regular road shipments; however, road transport is heavily undermined by institutional, procedural, and infrastructural problems along NELTI routes.

The TRACECA is a European Union technical assistance program aimed at strengthening economic relations, trade, and transport communication in the regions of the Black Sea basin, South Caucasus, and Central Asia. Signed in 1998 by Armenia, Azerbaijan, Bulgaria, Georgia, Kazakhstan, the Kyrgyz Republic, Moldova, Romania, Tajikistan, Turkey, Ukraine, and Uzbekistan, it consists of 22 road and rail routes and 12 ports.

The UNECE is a multilateral platform that facilitates greater economic integration and cooperation among its 56 member countries. Its main initiatives include the Euro-Asian Transport Links (EATL) project, the UN Special Program for the Economies of Central Asia (SPECA), and the related Aid for Trade initiative. Among other programs, UNECE has been involved in implementation of the Almaty Programme of Action, the implementation of the Transports Internationaux Routiers (TIR) convention, the harmonization of transport regulations and promotion of international transport networks, and the development of the freight village concept, as well as the facilitation of member countries' participation in the work of the Inland Transport Committee (European Commission 2012).

## Reference

European Commission. 2012. *Potential for Eurasia Land Bridge Corridors & Logistics Developments along the Corridors.* Brussels.

# Logistics Performance Index

The Logistics Performance Index (LPI), developed by the World Bank (World Bank 2007, 2010, 2012), is one of the key means to compare countries' performance in international supply chains. The LPI is based on the assessment of logistics professionals located in a country's major trading partners and is a weighted average of these six components:

1. Efficiency of the customs (border) clearance process
2. Quality of trade and transport-related infrastructure
3. Ease of arranging competitively priced international shipments
4. Competence and quality of logistics services
5. Ability to track and trace consignments
6. Timeliness: Frequency with which shipments reach the consignee within the scheduled or expected time.

The indicators 1, 2, and 4 refer to inputs to logistics performance (see figure B.1), and the other three proxy the supply-chain performance outcomes in costs, delays, and reliability. The scores are on a 1 (worst) to 5 (best) scale.

The survey also pools information collected from the same professionals on their own countries. It includes detailed information on the logistics environment, core logistics processes, institutions, and performance time and cost data. It has the following components:

1. Quality of trade-related infrastructure
2. Competence of service providers
3. Efficiency of border procedures.

The LPI has had three editions: 2007, 2010, and 2012. A fourth edition will be published in March 2014. Table 2.5 gives the most recent results (from 2012).

**Figure B.1  Input and Output Logistics Performance Index Indicators**

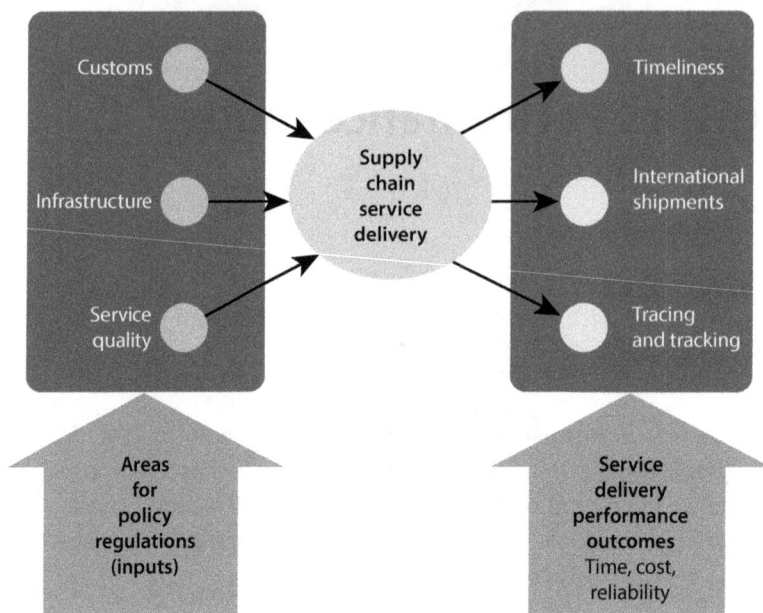

Source: World Bank 2012.

## References

Arvis, Jean-François. 2010. *The Cost of Being Landlocked: Logistics Costs and Supply Chain Reliability.* Directions in Development 558837. Washington, DC: World Bank.

———. 2013. *Trade Costs in the Developing World.* World Bank, Washington, DC.

World Bank. 2007. *Connecting to Compete 2007: Trade Logistics in the Global Economy.* World Bank, Washington, DC.

———. 2010. *Connecting to Compete 2010: Trade Logistics in the Global Economy.* World Bank, Washington, DC.

———. 2012. *Connecting to Compete: Trade Logistics in the Global Economy 2012.* World Bank, Washington, DC.

# Time and Cost of Transport by Road and Rail

**Figure C.1  Time and Cost of Transport by Road and Rail**

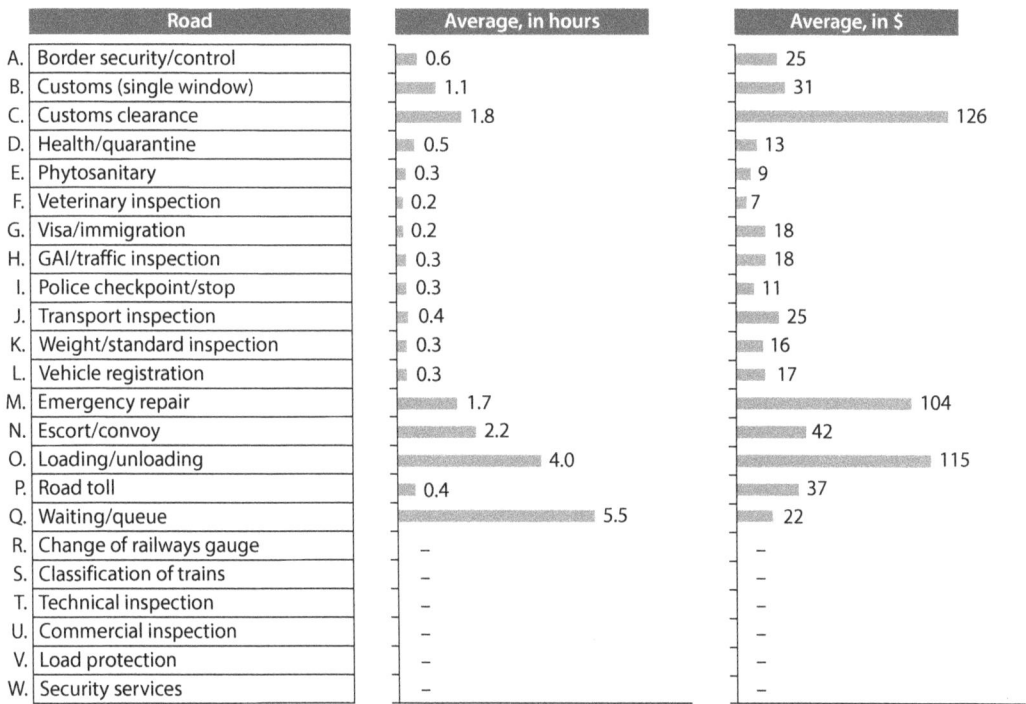

| | Road | Average, in hours | Average, in $ |
|---|---|---|---|
| A. | Border security/control | 0.6 | 25 |
| B. | Customs (single window) | 1.1 | 31 |
| C. | Customs clearance | 1.8 | 126 |
| D. | Health/quarantine | 0.5 | 13 |
| E. | Phytosanitary | 0.3 | 9 |
| F. | Veterinary inspection | 0.2 | 7 |
| G. | Visa/immigration | 0.2 | 18 |
| H. | GAI/traffic inspection | 0.3 | 18 |
| I. | Police checkpoint/stop | 0.3 | 11 |
| J. | Transport inspection | 0.4 | 25 |
| K. | Weight/standard inspection | 0.3 | 16 |
| L. | Vehicle registration | 0.3 | 17 |
| M. | Emergency repair | 1.7 | 104 |
| N. | Escort/convoy | 2.2 | 42 |
| O. | Loading/unloading | 4.0 | 115 |
| P. | Road toll | 0.4 | 37 |
| Q. | Waiting/queue | 5.5 | 22 |
| R. | Change of railways gauge | – | – |
| S. | Classification of trains | – | – |
| T. | Technical inspection | – | – |
| U. | Commercial inspection | – | – |
| V. | Load protection | – | – |
| W. | Security services | – | – |

*figure continues next page*

**Figure C.1  Time and Cost of Transport by Road and Rail** *(continued)*

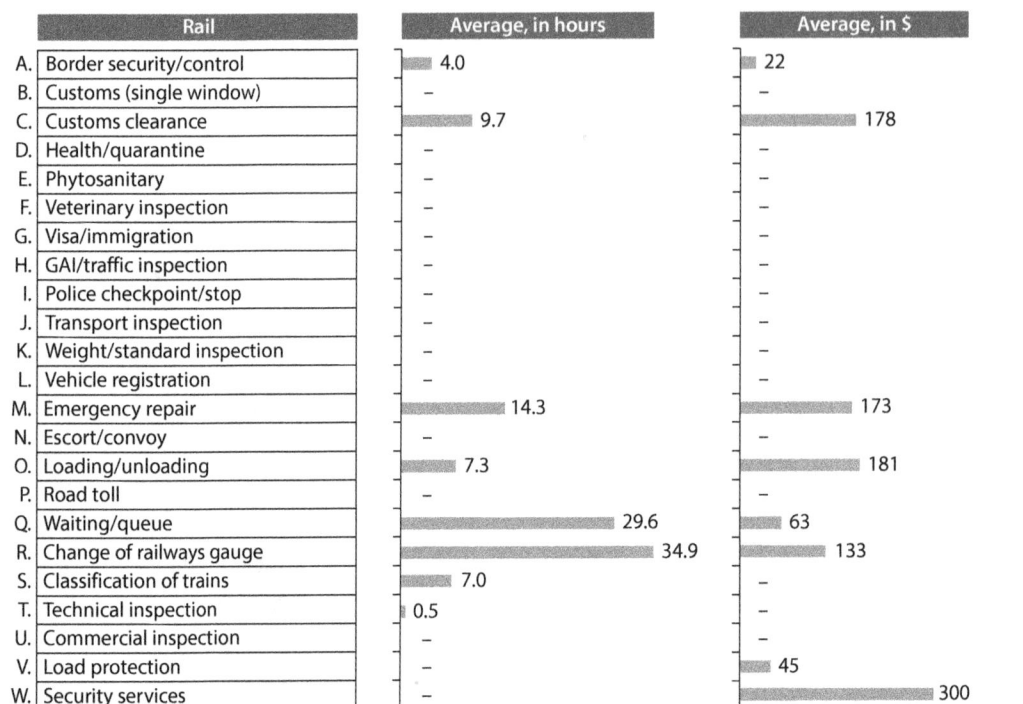

| Rail | Average, in hours | Average, in $ |
|------|------------------|---------------|
| A. Border security/control | 4.0 | 22 |
| B. Customs (single window) | – | – |
| C. Customs clearance | 9.7 | 178 |
| D. Health/quarantine | – | – |
| E. Phytosanitary | – | – |
| F. Veterinary inspection | – | – |
| G. Visa/immigration | – | – |
| H. GAI/traffic inspection | – | – |
| I. Police checkpoint/stop | – | – |
| J. Transport inspection | – | – |
| K. Weight/standard inspection | – | – |
| L. Vehicle registration | – | – |
| M. Emergency repair | 14.3 | 173 |
| N. Escort/convoy | – | – |
| O. Loading/unloading | 7.3 | 181 |
| P. Road toll | – | – |
| Q. Waiting/queue | 29.6 | 63 |
| R. Change of railways gauge | 34.9 | 133 |
| S. Classification of trains | 7.0 | – |
| T. Technical inspection | 0.5 | – |
| U. Commercial inspection | – | – |
| V. Load protection | – | 45 |
| W. Security services | – | 300 |

*Source:* ADB 2009–2012.

**Table C.1  Average Road Carriage Prices from Main Markets**
*US cents/ton-km*

| Country of origin | To | Distance, km | Average trucking rate US¢/ton-km | To Kazakhstan, on average Min | To Kazakhstan, on average Max |
|-------------------|-----|------|------|-----|------|
| Import from Germany | Kazakhstan | 6,906 | 7.1 | 4.8 | 15.4 |
| Import from Lithuania (Vilnius) | Almaty | 4,780 | 7.0 | 5.9 | 8.3 |
| Import from Russia (Moscow) | Almaty | 4,020 | 6.4 | 4.5 | 9.9 |
| Import from Russia (Saint Petersburg) | Almaty | 2,129 | 6.5 | 4.5 | 9.9 |
| Import from Russia (Novosibirsk) | Almaty | 1,754 | 4.5 | 4.5 | 9.9 |
| Import from Turkey (Istanbul) | Almaty | 5,615 | 13.1 | 9.0 | 18.2 |
| Import from Ukraine (Kharkov) | Almaty | 3,744 | 9.1 | 3.8 | 20.2 |
| Import from China (Urumchi) | Kazakhstan | 665.4 | 21.2 | 4.0 | 39.7 |

*Source:* Expert interviews and web-based transportation marketplaces in Kazakhstan.

## Reference

ADB (Asian Development Bank). 2009–12. *CAREC Corridors Performance: Measurement and Monitoring.* Annual Reports, ADB, Manila.

# Examples of Road Freight Transportation Prices to and from Main Markets of the Kyrgyz Republic, February–March 2012

| From | | To | | Type | m³ | Tons | Distance (km) | $ | $/km | US¢/ton-km |
|------|---|-----|---|------|-----|------|------|------|------|------|
| Bishkek | KG | Ekaterinburg | RU | Tilt | 86 | 20 | 2,520 | 3,300 | 1.3 | 6.5 |
| Tokmak | KG | Moscow | RU | Tilt | 60 | 20 | 4,061 | 2,000 | 0.5 | 2.5 |
| Bishkek | KG | Khujand | TJ | Tilt | 86 | 30 | 770 | 2,457 | 3.2 | 10.6 |
| Bishkek | KG | Moscow | RU | Tilt | 86 | 4 | 3,599 | 2,500 | 0.7 | 17.4 |
| Bishkek | KG | Moscow | RU | Tilt | 86 | 20 | 3,599 | 4,000 | 1.1 | 5.6 |
| Bishkek | KG | Novosibirsk | RU | Tilt | 86 | 20 | 2,101 | 5,500 | 2.6 | 13.1 |
| Bishkek | KG | Moscow | RU | Tilt | 86 | 20 | 3,599 | 3,300 | 0.9 | 4.6 |
| Bishkek | KG | Moscow | RU | Tilt | 86 | 20 | 3,599 | 3,500 | 1.0 | 4.9 |
| Bishkek | KG | Riga | LV | Tilt | 86 | 20 | 4,648 | 3,000 | 0.6 | 3.2 |
| Bishkek | KG | Amsterdam | NL | Tilt | 86 | 20 | 6,175 | 3,950 | 0.6 | 3.2 |
| Bishkek | KG | Berlin | DE | Tilt | 86 | 20 | 5,600 | 3,360 | 0.6 | 3.0 |
| Bishkek | KG | Munich | DE | Tilt | 86 | 20 | 5,950 | 4,590 | 0.8 | 3.9 |
| Bishkek | KG | Paris | FR | Tilt | 86 | 20 | 6,550 | 4,600 | 0.7 | 3.5 |
| Bishkek | KG | Hamburg | DE | Tilt | 86 | 20 | 5,850 | 4,585 | 0.8 | 3.9 |
| Bishkek | KG | Hamburg | DE | Tilt | 86 | 20 | 5,850 | 5,900 | 1.0 | 5.0 |
| Bishkek | KG | Istanbul | TK | Tilt | 86 | 20 | 5,233 | 4,500 | 0.9 | 4.3 |
| Bishkek | KG | Tehran | IR | Box | 86 | 20 | 2,800 | 8,500 | 0.3 | 1.6 |
| Chelyabinsk | RU | Bishkek | KG | Tilt | 11 | 2.7 | 2,229 | 3,000 | 1.3 | 49.8 |
| St. Petersburg | RU | Bishkek | KG | Tilt | 110 | 25 | 4,642 | 6,990 | 1.5 | 6.0 |
| Novosibirsk | RU | Bishkek | KG | Tilt | 86 | 20 | 2,101 | 3,500 | 1.7 | 8.3 |
| Chelyabinsk | RU | Bishkek | KG | Tilt | 86 | 20 | 2,229 | 2,000 | 0.9 | 4.5 |
| St. Petersburg | RU | Bishkek | KG | Tilt | 25 | 3.3 | 4,642 | 5,500 | 1.2 | 35.9 |
| Moscow | RU | Bishkek | KG | Tilt | 86 | 20 | 3,599 | 3,500 | 1.0 | 4.9 |

*table continues next page*

**Appendix D** (*continued*)

| From | | To | | Type | $m^3$ | Tons | Distance (km) | $ | $/km | US¢/ton-km |
|---|---|---|---|---|---|---|---|---|---|---|
| St. Petersburg | RU | Bishkek | KG | Tilt | 86 | 20 | 4,642 | 7,500 | 1.6 | 8.1 |
| Omsk | RU | Bishkek | KG | Tilt | 86 | 20 | 1,715 | 3,714 | 2.2 | 10.8 |
| St. Petersburg | RU | Bishkek | KG | Tilt | 86 | 20 | 4,642 | 7,500 | 1.6 | 8.1 |
| Ekaterinburg | RU | Osh | KG | Tilt | 120 | 20 | 2,904 | 4,215 | 1.5 | 7.3 |
| Samara | RU | Bishkek | kg | Tilt | 86 | 20 | 3,011 | 6,300 | 2.1 | 10.5 |
| Chelyabinsk | RU | Bishkek | KG | Tilt | 7 | 3 | 2,229 | 2,000 | 0.9 | 29.9 |
| Ekaterinburg | RU | Osh | KG | Tilt | 86 | 20 | 2,904 | 3,709 | 1.3 | 6.4 |
| Asha | RU | Bishkek | KG | Tilt | 40 | 10 | 2,986 | 1,686 | 0.6 | 5.6 |
| Moscow | RU | Bishkek | KG | Tilt | 86 | 20 | 3,599 | 6,000 | 1.7 | 8.3 |
| Moscow | RU | Bishkek | KG | Tilt | 86 | 20 | 3,599 | 6,000 | 1.7 | 8.3 |
| Ekaterinburg | RU | Osh | KG | Tilt | 10 | 5 | 2,900 | 2,717 | 0.9 | 18.7 |
| Kostanai | RU | Bishkek | KG | Tilt | 86 | 22 | 1,842 | 3,000 | 1.6 | 7.4 |
| Ekaterinburg | RU | Bishkek | KG | Tilt | 5 | 4 | 2,551 | 1,690 | 0.7 | 16.6 |
| Asha | RU | Bishkek | KG | Tilt | 5 | 10 | 2,569 | 1,690 | 0.7 | 6.6 |
| Almaty | KZ | Bishkek | KG | Tilt | 5 | 5 | 323 | 703 | 2.2 | 43.5 |
| Moscow | RU | Bishkek | KG | Tilt | 86 | 20 | 3,599 | 7,000 | 1.9 | 9.7 |
| Novosibirsk | RU | Bishkek | KG | Tilt | 86 | 20 | 2,101 | 6,000 | 2.9 | 14.3 |
| Moscow | RU | Bishkek | KG | Tilt | 86 | 20 | 3,599 | 6,000 | 1.7 | 8.3 |
| St. Petersburg | RU | Bishkek | KG | Box | 86 | 20 | 4,642 | 7,000 | 1.5 | 7.5 |
| Moscow | RU | Bishkek | KG | Tilt | 86 | 20 | 3,599 | 7,000 | 1.9 | 9.7 |
| Riga | LV | Bishkek | KG | Tilt | 86 | 20 | 4,648 | 9,430 | 2.0 | 10.1 |
| Amsterdam | NL | Bishkek | KG | Tilt | 86 | 20 | 6,175 | 10,500 | 1.7 | 8.5 |
| Berlin | DE | Bishkek | KG | Tilt | 86 | 20 | 5,600 | 8,900 | 1.6 | 7.9 |
| Munich | DE | Bishkek | KG | Tilt | 86 | 20 | 5,950 | 9,700 | 1.6 | 8.2 |
| Paris | FR | Bishkek | KG | Tilt | 86 | 20 | 6,550 | 12,500 | 1.9 | 9.5 |
| Hamburg | DE | Bishkek | KG | Tilt | 86 | 20 | 5,850 | 10,300 | 1.8 | 8.8 |
| Bishkek | KG | St. Petersburg | RU | Box | 86 | 20 | 4,642 | 3,500 | 0.8 | 3.8 |
| Hamburg | DE | Bishkek | KG | Tilt | 86 | 20 | 5,850 | 11,800 | 2.0 | 10.1 |
| Istanbul | TK | Bishkek | KG | Tilt | 86 | 20 | 5,233 | 12,000 | 2.3 | 11.5 |

*Source:* Expert interviews, available web sources.

# Examples of Road Freight Transportation Prices to and from Main Markets of Tajikistan, February 2012

| From | | To | | Type | $m^3$ | Tons | Market | Distance (km) | $ | $/km |
|------|---|-----|---|------|------|------|--------|--------------|---|------|
| Dushanbe | TJ | Moscow | RU | Tilt | 86 | 20 | Export to CIS | 3,864 | 5,000 | 1.3 |
| Dushanbe | TJ | Moscow | RU | Tilt | 86 | 20 | Export to CIS | 3,864 | 4,500 | 1.2 |
| Dushanbe | TJ | Berlin | DE | Tilt | 86 | 20 | Export to EU | 5,693 | 3,000 | 0.5 |
| Dushanbe | TJ | Munich | DE | Tilt | 86 | 20 | Export to EU | 6,078 | 7,920 | 1.3 |
| Dushanbe | TJ | Istanbul | TR | Tilt | 86 | 20 | Export to other | 4,618 | 3,000 | 0.6 |
| Istanbul | TR | Dushanbe | TJ | Tilt | 86 | 20 | Import from TR | 4,618 | 12,000 | 2.6 |
| Moscow | RU | Dushanbe | TJ | Tilt | 86 | 20 | Import from CIS | 3,864 | 6,900 | 1.8 |
| Moscow | RU | Dushanbe | TJ | Tilt | 86 | 20 | Import from CIS | 3,864 | 8,500 | 2.2 |
| Moscow | RU | Dushanbe | TJ | Tilt | 86 | 20 | Import from CIS | 3,864 | 9,000 | 2.3 |
| Kiev | UA | Dushanbe | TJ | Tilt | 100 | 20 | Import from CIS | 4,275 | 6,700 | 1.6 |
| Slavuta | UA | Dushanbe | TJ | Tilt | 120 | 15 | Import from CIS | 6,428 | 7,000 | 1.1 |
| Dnepropetrovsk | UA | Dushanbe | TJ | Tilt | 96 | 19.5 | Import from CIS | 3,989 | 7,000 | 1.8 |
| Vinnitsa | UA | Dushanbe | TJ | Tilt | 86 | 20 | Import from CIS | 5,279 | 5,000 | 0.9 |
| Dnepropetrovsk | UA | Dushanbe | TJ | Tilt | 100 | 19.5 | Import from CIS | 3,989 | 7,200 | 1.8 |
| Kiev | UA | Dushanbe | TJ | Tilt | 86 | 20 | Import from CIS | 4,413 | 7,500 | 1.7 |
| Almaty | KZ | Khujand | TJ | Tilt | 86 | 20 | Intra-CIS | 1,168 | 3,000 | 2.6 |
| Kiev | UA | Dushanbe | TJ | Tilt | 86 | 20 | Import from CIS | 4,413 | 6,700 | 1.5 |
| Moscow | RU | Dushanbe | TJ | Tilt | 86 | 20 | Import from CIS | 4,366 | 6,900 | 1.6 |
| Berlin | DE | Dushanbe | TJ | Tilt | 86 | 20 | Import from EU | 5,693 | 10,560 | 1.9 |
| Przemysl | PL | Dushanbe | TJ | Tilt | 86 | 20 | Import from EU | 4,901 | 11,220 | 2.3 |
| Berlin | DE | Dushanbe | TJ | Tilt | 86 | 20 | Import from EU | 5,693 | 15,840 | 2.8 |
| Munich | DE | Dushanbe | TJ | Tilt | 86 | 20 | Import from EU | 6,078 | 14,520 | 2.4 |

*Source:* Expert interviews, available web sources.

www.ingramcontent.com/pod-product-compliance
Lightning Source LLC
Chambersburg PA
CBHW080617270326
41928CB00016B/3099